PERVERSION:
A JUNGIAN APPROACH

PERVERSION:
A JUNGIAN APPROACH

Fiona Ross

Routledge
Taylor & Francis Group

LONDON AND NEW YORK

First published 2013 by Karnac Books Ltd.

Published 2018 by Routledge
2 Park Square, Milton Park, Abingdon, Oxon OX14 4RN
711 Third Avenue, New York, NY 10017, USA

Routledge is an imprint of the Taylor & Francis Group, an informa business

British Library Cataloguing in Publication Data

A C.I.P. for this book is available from the British Library

  ISBN 9781780490304 (pbk)

Edited, designed and produced by The Studio Publishing Services Ltd
www.publishingservicesuk.co.uk
e-mail: studio@publishingservicesuk.co.uk

CONTENTS

ABOUT THE AUTHOR

Dr Fiona Ross is a Jungian analyst, a professional member of the Society of Analytical Psychology, and a chartered psychologist. She works in private practice in London and has many years teaching experience of analysis and psychotherapy. She is author of *Understanding Perversion in Clinical Practice: Structure and Strategy in the Psyche* (Karnac, 2003). Her MA dissertation examined *The Internalized Victim— Perpetrator Relationship*. She continued her research into perversion with a doctoral thesis on Jungian contributions to the theory of perversion.

To those whose inner turmoil elicits no sympathy

CHAPTER ONE

Setting the scene

What art thou that usurp'st this time of night?

Shakespeare, *Hamlet*, Act 1: Scene 1

Psycho-analysis and analytical psychology as opposing interpretive traditions

Theories of perversion have traditionally belonged within the Freudian interpretive tradition, which I refer to as psycho-analysis (with a hyphen), freeing psychoanalysis (without a hyphen) to denote the whole analytic field including analytical psychology. Freud's theories of psychosexual development are cornerstones of an architecture of the unconscious mind in which perversion is portrayed as the shadow lurking beyond the limits of mature, healthy functioning, helping to define the parameters of normality. Although perversion has this significant position, its meaning has been narrowly developed in psycho-analytical theory since it almost exclusively refers to sexual perversion, highlighting the prominence given to sexuality more generally in Freudian psychology.

Freud, Jung, and reality

I agree with Roncaglia (2007, p. 24) that "our knowledge and experience cannot consist of an objective appraisal of external reality", as is sometimes claimed in traditional science, and that "The truth of the world varies according to the various perspectives from which it is viewed" (Hauke, 2000, p. 252). This concurs with Jung's psychological rule that everything psychic is relative and there is no objective truth in psychology because of the personal differences of observers (Bair, 2003, p. 286). Such a view respects situated experience (human inquiry) (McLeod, 2001), and recognises different interpretive traditions, and different footings (personal positions), while accepting that the "footing of the objective observer may be masking their own links to the data presented" (Branney, 2006, p. 2). In this light, theory is "a way of looking at the world, and not a form of knowledge of how the world is" (Bohm, 1983, pp. 3–4).

Spence asserts that, "The force of psychoanalytic argument has traditionally relied rather more on rhetorical persuasion than on appeal to the data" (Spence, 1982, p. 43). Giving some credence to this claim, my aim is to adopt an ethnographic approach considering any theorist's viewpoint as embedded within its cultural context. My aim is to accept theoretical pluralism and not to privilege one interpretive tradition or attempt to disprove any particular theoretical perspective. The making of certain ontological and epistemological assumptions is inevitable, and the approach I have taken is that a particular theory arises through the need to find a perspective that enables understanding, and without which the object of concern might be lost from the theorist's view.

Psycho-analysis and analytic psychology are shared cultures, but also counter-cultures that disrupt each other, providing an important methodological tool. The introduction of a Jungian perspective is intended to re-contextualise the concept of perversion so that it can profitably be reexamined without the stranglehold of its psycho-analytic roots.

Theory is conceived through the imaginative relationship between theorist and reality. Although both Freud and Jung might agree that A comes before B and C usually follows; as two people with quite different personalities, their perceptions and interpretations of what happens between A and B or B and C might be strikingly dissimilar. The roots of disharmony between Jungian and Freudian theoretical perspectives lie in incompatible aspects of their originators' divergent creativities. Within Jung's typology framework, Jung himself is an introvert. He is absorbed by the inner, including inner logic. His "artistic personality" is best captured factor-analytically by strength in an "Openness to Experience" dimension, a trait characterised by aesthetic sensitivity, intellectual curiosity, imagination, and innovative striving (Chamorro-Premuzic, Furnham, & Reimers, 2007, p. 85). Jung would agree with Hillman's positioning of the psychotherapist as "*the attendant of the soul*" (Hillman, 1964, p. 116). By contrast, Freud is an extraverted thinker, turning his thinking function outward to his perception of the world. Whereas Freud wants to know, Jung wants to experience unknowing. As Casement observes, "The main emphasis for [Jung] lies in *experience*, which centres on religious experience based on inner reality deeply felt not on rational or dogmatic theory" (Casement, 2001, p. 41). Jung is influenced by Kant who divides knowledge into the phenomenal world, known through cognition, and the neumenal world which is not. The "thing-in-itself" of the neumenal world is timeless, spaceless, and causeless, within and without the psyche. While Jung claims he is an empiricist who relies for his theorising "on the evidence of inner experience" (Casement, 2001, p. 39), Freud aspires to the objectivity of medicine and the physical sciences. This means that Freudian theory allies itself to a tradition that is more easily accepted as the orthodox doctrine, encouraging other psycho-analytic theorists to work intratextually, cross-referencing Freudian concepts rather than looking beyond them. As Hogensen observes, "Freud's system presents a unique theory of interpretation in that once one engages his theory it is almost impossible to step back out of its constraints and assess the phenomena independently" (Hogenson, 1994, p. ix). Put more dramatically, Steele believes that Freud and Jung live "in different realities" and psycho-analysis and analytical psychology "are two world-views in collision" (Steele, 1982, p. 314), with Freud believing in "external reality" and Jung in "psychic reality" (1982, p. 314). Jung's consciousness is not about material objects, but the world of psychic images, material reality to him is just a hypothesis. By contrast, Freud's hermeneutic is reason, not experience (Steele, 1982, p. 323).

Both accept the cultural norms of their time giving men, who represent rational thought and intellect, a commanding position over women, yet Jung insistently values the feminine, as the balancing opposite that should always be included. If Freud represents excess of thinking to Jung, then conversely, Jung represents the irrational "feminine" quality of intuition to Freud. If we add to this Freud's sexual interpretation of penis envy in the female, an antagonism arises in which Freud's theory of perversion is associated for Jung with Freud's excess of masculinity. It is then incumbent upon Jung to redress this imbalance through a "feminist" privileging of those aspects of his own theory that represent the irrational, the "theory without a penis". This might naturally lead to a reduction in emphasis on sexuality and an almost total exclusion of perversion, traditionally considered to be a masculine psychopathology.

This omission has been a consistent trend in analytical psychology. Despite Eiguer's observation that "Perversion has been on hand at every critical point in the development of psychoanalysis" (Eiguer, 1999, p. 671), it is conspicuously lacking in analytical psychology. Of the thirteen references to perversion(s) in the *General Index of Jung's Collected Works* (Read, Fordham, Adler, & McGuire, 1979, p. 520), four are passing references, two use the term perversion as description by analogy (animus perversion, intellectual perversion), one refers to homosexuality (an *in*version to Freud), four are introduced only to criticise Freudian theory, one refers to "bad habits" (Jung, 1916a, par. 560), one grudgingly accepts the term in infancy, and one suggests dropping the term altogether. Similarly, *The Journal of Analytical Psychology* also under-represents the subject of perversion. Although between 1955 and 2008 there are eighty-three papers which include the word perversion at least once, most of these are passing references. Only seven papers address sexual perversion making some links with Jungian theory (a further one refers to homosexuality), whereas eleven use the term in a non-sexual context, all referring in some sense to perversion of mental processes, such as higher consciousness, learning, ethical attitude, or linguistic expression. There is little basis in this literature for expanding on current theory from a Jungian perspective.

To be fair to the profession, there has been some acknowledgement within psycho-analysis that the definition of perversion may be too constrictive (Laplanche & Pontalis, 1973, pp. 306–307), but this idea is not comprehensively developed. Chapter Five begins to build on existing support for broadening the concept to encompass more than sexual perversion by including perverse ideation and behaviour that is not manifestly sexual (Fogel & Myers, 1991; Laplanche & Pontalis,

1973, p. 307; Morgenthaler, 1988, p. 13; Phillips, 1994, p. 65; Waddell & Williams, 1991, pp. 203–213).

Part of the difficulty of defining perversion and deciding whether it is sexual or not, lies in the difficulty of defining sexuality itself. In his *Introductory Lectures on Psycho-analysis* (1916–1917), Freud grapples with the meaning of the term "sexual", concluding that it appropriately defines everything which is concerned with obtaining bodily pleasure (Dreher, 2000, pp. 9–10; Freud, 1916–1917, pp. 303–304). This definition is too broad for Jung, who avoids defining sexuality, but moves to strike out Freud's sexual definition of libido, and insists that "the libido of the child is occupied far more with subsidiary functions of a mental and physical nature than with local sexual functions" (Jung, 1913, par. 268). Their differences highlight a grey area between sexual and non-sexual perversion, an area that I call "bodily perversion" since it relates to behaviour that has a significant bodily focus that might or might not be regarded as sexual, depending on how broadly sexuality is defined. Jung's view of sexuality, being narrower than Freud's, allows for this area of bodily action that is perverse but not obviously sexual.

As this ambiguous region has not been developed, it offers an opportunity for the beginnings of an expansion of the concept of perversion since, on the one hand it borders on sexual perversion without falling clearly into any accepted definition, while on the other, it refers to bodily intercourse that is not obviously sexual in aim and so could be classified as non-sexual. In Chapter Seven, I present an example of recurrent compulsion to administer a lethal injection into the body of another person. The aim is not sexual, at least in the narrowest sense of the term, but is, in my view, perverse in that it has the essential qualities of addiction, compulsion, vengefulness, self-deception, splitting, projection, and regression. These are all qualities described in Chapter Four as characteristic of sexual perversion. But I also wish to extend the concept of perversion further, to include behaviours that are not body focused.

I maintain that activities that are not ostensibly sexual but, like sexual perversion, reflect a perverse aim, fixation on an inappropriate object, and are rigid, compulsive, and addictive, can legitimately be described as perversions. These are "non-sexual perversions", emanating like sexual perversions from a perverse psychic structure. Broadening the understanding of perversion in this way relegates the adjective "sexual" from its standing as the defining quality of perversion to being characteristic of only one type of perverse manifestation.

Analytical psychology provides a comprehensive theoretical model through which such expansion of the concept of perversion can be supported. Specifically this will be shown in Chapters Six and Seven to involve adoption of a broader understanding of the concept of libido, extending beyond the area of sexuality; linking of instinct through the collective unconscious to imagery and perceptive ideas; the acceptance of archetypal governance in psychic organisation and in defence mechanisms; and understanding of a futural sense in the psyche, including teleological directness in the creation of symptoms. These expansions require the integration of a Jungian perspective within the traditional model of perversion so that the concept describes a quality of human relationship and not just of sexuality.

The aim of this book is to revise the psycho-analytic model through the introduction of Jungian concepts that extend the understanding of perversion beyond the bounds of sexuality to a more general relational context. Opportunities for this expansion begin in Chapter Three with the etymological exploration of the word perversion. Usage in religious, moral, sociological, and legal contexts reveals a wide swath of meanings within which only a thin stripe illuminates the traditional theories of perversion adopted in psychoanalysis.

Expanding the width of this stripe is my first step in building an interpretive framework for both sexual and non-sexual perversion. Perversion, in this broader sense, covers a range of psychic processes with associated behaviours, including, but extending beyond, the area of sexuality. My theoretical formulation, expounded in Chapter Seven, includes Jungian concepts and gives perversion a clear position within the theory of analytical psychology, where the concept has been neglected, as well as contributing to its understanding in psychoanalysis where perversion, despite some post-Freudian developments, traditionally relates to sexuality.

Definitions of perversion

Freudian definition

In the first of his *Three Essays on the Theory of Sexuality* (1905d), Freud defines perversions as "sexual activities which either (a) extend, in an anatomical sense, beyond the regions of the body that are designed for sexual union, or (b) linger over the immediate relations to the sexual object which should normally be traversed rapidly on the path towards the final sexual aim" (Freud, 1905d, p. 165). (a) refers to deviations in the sexual aim from heterosexual genitality and (b) to deviations in the sexual object from an adult of the opposite sex. By defining perversions behaviourally as "sexual activities", Freud links the internal psychic "aim" with the external "object"; a link which I retain. In post-Freudian extensions to the definition, the term has also been used to describe "a character trait, a relational style and a type of transference" (Filippini, 2005, p. 758).

Diagnostic and Statistical Manual *definition*

The third edition of the *Diagnostic and Statistical Manual of Mental Disorders* (*DSM-III*) (American Psychiatric Association, 1980) replaces "perversion" with the less emotive term "paraphilia". The latest edition, *DSM-IV* (American Psychiatric Association, 2000), continues a classificatory approach to identifying sexual perversion through behavioural symptoms. It lists eight main behavioural categories: exhibitionism, fetishism, frotteurism, paedophilia, sexual masochism, sexual sadism, transvestic fetishism, and voyeurism, then adds a category for paraphilias that do not meet the criteria for any of the specific categories, including telephone scatologia (obscene phone calls), necrophilia (corpses), partialism (exclusive focus on part of body), zoophilia (animals), coprophilia (faeces), klismaphilia (enemas), and urophilia (urine) (2000, pp. 569–576). This list will evolve as society develops in the observation and understanding of sexual behaviour regarded as deviant. For example, gerontophilia, like paedophilia, now describes unusual sexual attraction to a specific age range—in this case the elderly. Stalking motivated by sexual fantasies might also be described as a sexual perversion. Stalking can even be subdivided since cyber stalking is now thought to be more common than proximal stalking and to be psychologically different judging from the high proportion (about forty per cent) of male victims targeted: although cyber stalking might be either a prelude or adjunct to proximal stalking (McVeigh, 2011).

There are three further defining features of paraphilia: "recurrent, intense sexually arousing fantasies, sexual urges, or behaviours

generally involving 1) nonhuman objects, 2) the suffering or humiliation of oneself or one's partner, or 3) children or other nonconsenting
persons that occur over a period of at least 6 months" (American
Psychiatric Association, 2000, p. 566).

My extended definition

Due to the dearth of Jungian literature on the subject, there is no established or agreed Jungian definition of perversion. I do not intend to
promote an exclusively Jungian model of perversion but to expand
the traditional psycho-analytic model to include a Jungian perspective
and Jungian theory. I define perversion as intrapsychic deception
enacted relationally in the outside world. I consider perversion to
result from early relational trauma and to include vengeful behavioural enactments, not necessarily sexual, that have become addictive
and are symptomatic of a particular type of defensive psychic structure that establishes and perpetuates self-deception through the
employment of a variety of defence mechanisms, particularly splitting, projection, and regression. I understand all perversion to include
behavioural enactment, and all relationships, even symbolic relationships with inanimate objects, to be templated by kleptocratic imagery
and ideation. (Kleptocracy is government by thieves, or a thieves
regime). In other words, all relationships are approached as opportunities for exploitation and theft, including psychological theft.

CHAPTER TWO

Rationale for the structure of the book

Find where truth is hid though it were hid indeed within the centre

Shakespeare, *Hamlet*, Act 2: Scene 2

Theories of perversion have fallen into untested ways of defining the concept. My aim is to undertake a comparative and conceptual analysis, with illustrations outside the clinic setting, rather than collecting additional clinical data. The material introduced from the fields of psycho-analysis and analytical psychology is largely conceptual, aimed at comparing and advancing ways of looking at perversion rather than extending knowledge in the empirical sense of accumulating additional factual material (Dreher, 2000, p. 23). It is assumed that, through the "privileged competence [that] belongs to the analyst" (Spence, 1982, p. 44), concepts in the psychoanalytic field have been derived from empirical data through induction, or have been abstracted from other conceptualisations which were at some stage derived from empirical data, and so have become an aggregate of single-case research.

Certain exemptions are made in this book. My understanding of perversion is that it is a mode of relating that crosses the boundaries of sexual orientation. Therefore homosexuality, which Freud regards as an inversion rather than a perversion, and which has been excluded from *The Diagnostic and Statistical Manual of Mental Disorders* (American Psychiatric Association, 2000) since 1973, is regarded as a sexual orientation, not a sexual perversion. I exclude specific reference to women. This is partly because much of the published theory on perversion focuses on men, but also because of differences in the relationship of perverse psychic structure and bodily action between men and women. These have been addressed elsewhere, particularly by female writers (Kaplan, 1991; McDougall, 1995; Welldon, 1988), but are beyond the scope of this book. However, the espoused theoretical model does also apply to women, although further explanation would be necessary to position women in relation to the theory.

Dreher (2000, p. 16) suggests four thematic divisions for clarifying a concept; investigation of (i) origin, (ii) history, (iii) current use, and finally (iv) critical discussion possibly leading to a different use of the concept. I plan to follow a similar, but not identical, pattern, with relevant literature introduced and considered within each theme (Cooper, 1989, in Moustakas, 1994, p. 112).

The next chapter, Chapter Three, addresses Dreher's first theme, origin. The origin of the term perversion is examined before its use in early psychiatry as well as outside the psychiatric sphere. My intention at this stage is to examine the breadth and variance in meaning of the term, much of which is jettisoned as historical baggage when the concept enters psycho-analysis. For my purposes, these early meanings can usefully be revisited. Perversion is shown as a stigmatising word, intimately bound with the ascendancy of certain groups in society and their ability to use the concept to label and exclude. This emphasises the historical power imbalance in perverse relationships and helps to explain how theories of perversion often adopt the reversible abusive parent/child, or perpetrator/victim model (Mogenson, 2005, p. 80). This model, seen in reverse, or with the understanding of unconscious processes, also points to the perpetrator's own victimisation through past experiences of abuse or neglect leading to problems in making and maintaining reciprocal relationships. The understanding of an imbalance of power, destructively reversed, is integral to my own formulation of perversion, for which these earlier meanings provide building blocks.

Chapter Four then examines the history (Dreher's second theme) and meaning of the concept of sexual perversion within psychoanalysis, with contributions from Freudian and post-Freudian theorists grouped thematically around the qualities that have been identified as characteristic of sexual perversion. Broad areas of theoretical agreement are summarised. I also look, in Chapter Five at movements within psycho-analysis towards broadening the concept to include non-sexual perversion, addressing Dreher's third theme of current use.

The main thrust of this book falls within the bounds of Dreher's final theme, involving the discussion and further expansion of the concept of perversion. Essential to this aim is the elucidation in Chapter Six of four major areas of conceptual difference between Freudian and Jungian interpretive traditions. From these it is possible to identify characteristic Jungian perspectives. In Chapter Seven, relevant aspects of these perspectives are combined with more traditional understandings of perversion to form an expanded theoretical model. Some concepts are also introduced from outside the analytic domain as they more clearly illustrate or illuminate particulars of the material addressed than do existing psychoanalytic concepts. New concepts are necessary to describe the functioning of the defence mechanisms of splitting, projection, and regression which are somewhat differently conceived in my formulation than in current psycho-analytic theory. Splitting is described as a two stage process which can be redeemed during the initial stage before a perverse psychic structure is established. Projection is linked to a generalised kleptocratic templating of experience that denies equality in relationship, and regression involves a process of psychic movement back to states of mind that predate personal experience. These processes are described more fully in Chapter Seven.

There are various possible ways to ground my theoretical formulation in the lives and psyches of human beings. The inclusion of first-hand clinical material, composite case illustrations, or secondary sources in the form of published psychoanalytic material, such as Freud's cases the "Rat Man" (Freud, 1909d) or Schreber (Freud, 1911a), are all possibilities, since they are already accompanied by extensive published material on unconscious processes and might be reinterpreted using my theoretical formulation. Although the "Rat Man" (Freud, 1909d) is identified by Freud as a case of obsessional neurosis, symptoms of fetishism and coprophilia are described and the case could be reinterpreted with the emphasis on sexual perversion. Both Grunberger (1966) and Lipton (1977) take this view. A reinterpretation of non-sexual perversion might be made in the case of Schreber, published by Freud (1911a) as a case of paranoia. Kaplan (1995) has already reinterpreted Schreber's behaviour as a perverse attempt to reinstate a bizarre relationship with his lost father. However, both cases lack the extensive detail that I require on the intricacies of behaviour outside the clinical setting that might be obtained from a more comprehensive life record. The inclusion of such outer life material is integral to my formulation since the perverse psychic structure is assumed to dominate all aspects of human functioning in both sexual and non-sexual perversion, including at the behavioural level. The core deceptive qualities of perversion also mean that a perverse patient's account (verbal behaviour) of his activities might be regarded as less credible than subjective material from a patient with non-perverse psychopathology.

Understanding of both the theoretical and practical implications of my theoretical formulation requires the comprehensive documentation of a person's behaviour in numerous life settings. This means that the argument propounded is better supported by detailed whole-life illustrations rather than by clinical material drawn from one particular mode of encounter with one other person. I therefore selected three detailed biographies of well known, famous, or infamous, individuals: Fred West (Burn, 1998), Harold Shipman (Peters, 2005), and Robert Maxwell (Thomas & Dillon, 2002). The use of biography highlights the need to include perversion as a quality of everyday life that can beneficially be considered outside the clinical setting. These biographical sources are used for illustrative purposes and are considered to resemble case studies in that the authors present detailed research on the lives of the biographees. Unlike psychoanalytic case studies, none of the authors has had an analytic, or even a personal relationship with their biographee and none of them sets out to present their biographee as perverse, so their material is less likely to be contaminated by presupposition. The biographies are accepted as presented by their authors, and can be interpreted to show varied manifestations of perverse psychic structure: one relates to sexual perversion involving sexual action; one to bodily perversion, with action that is taken against the body but does not appear to be primarily sexual; the third covers emotional and cognitive perversion, with similar psychic qualities but no manifest sexual intent.

I have no first-hand acquaintance with any of the subjects, so with all three biographies, the material is treated as if it were a case study, that is, as it is written and understood by the author. So it is *the biographer's account* of the biographee that is the illustrative material, rather than the biographee himself. It is an advantage that none of the authors demonstrates or states the intention of describing perversion. This material is obviously different from a clinical case study in which links are established and interpretations made between the patient's experiences and unconscious processes within the confines of the psychotherapeutic setting. The use of biography involves the linking of biographical events to subjective experience and the building of a body of substantiating biographical evidence, from different sources, for patterns of attitudes and behaviour on the part of the biographee throughout his life.

Short extracts from each biography are selected to illustrate every stage of the theoretical formulation. Adopting this approach, I could be accused of presenting an unrepresentative selection of extracts for the purposes of supporting my own theoretical standpoint. To demonstrate that the selections are representative of characteristic themes presented in the biography, a brief summary of each biography is given, emphasising the tone, the major character qualities highlighted, and the stance adopted by the biographer towards the biographee.

Obviously this method of understanding theory through biographical illustration is far from an evaluation through the hypothetical–deductive method commonly used in psychology. It is more akin to "inference to the best explanation" (IBE) (Haig, 2009). Haig describes this as a method used by both Darwin and Einstein, as "based on the idea that much of what we know about the world, in both science and everyday life, is based on considerations of the explanatory worth of our beliefs . . . IBE takes the relation between theory and evidence to be one of explanation, not logical entailment . . . IBE generally takes theory evaluation to be a predominantly qualitative exercise focussing on explanatory criteria rather than the quantitative assignment of probabilities to theories" (Haig, 2009, p. 948).

CHAPTER THREE

The length and breadth of the concept of perversion

Tragical—comical—historical—pastoral

Shakespeare, *Hamlet*, Act 2: Scene 2

T he term perversion is generally used to refer to a specific type of psychopathology identified by deviant forms of sexual behaviour. The aim of this chapter is to consider how such a particular perspective on perversion came about, by tracing the origins of the word perversion and exploring variation in use of the term, both before it enters the medical and psycho-analytic domains, and in other fields in which it has a specific, but not necessarily a sexual, meaning. Tracing the term historically demonstrates that perversion can and does have a wider meaning that narrowed when it was adopted by psycho-analysis.

An overview of the early history of perversion reveals a range of imminent or implicit ideas that might be usefully explored when considering a reshaping of the concept of perversion. My aim is to revert back to a broader meaning that incorporates many of the qualities described in this chapter, allowing perversion to be considered as a non-sexual as well as a sexual mode of relating. In Chapters Six and

Seven, I show that Jungian concepts are uniquely suited to expanding the psycho-analytic meaning of perversion to cover a far wider area of psychic functioning and of behaviour than sexuality alone, and that sacrificing a more general meaning in favour of a specifically sexual connotation, restricts the possibility of understanding the influence of a perverse psychic structure across all psychic functioning. There is also a risk that this under-inclusion leads to non-sexual perverse enactments being misunderstood through an interpretive framework that does not associate them with a perverse psychic structure.

Perversion is defined in the *Oxford English Dictionary* as, "The action of perverting or condition of being perverted; turning the wrong way; turning aside from truth or right; diversion of something from its original and proper course, state or meaning, corruption, distortion" (undated) (OED, 1989, p. 619). Explicit in this definition is the wrongness of perversion but there is also an implication of choice, of actively turning away from what is right. In the same dictionary the noun "pervert" is firstly defined as, "One who has been perverted; one who has forsaken a doctrine or system regarded as true for one esteemed false; an apostate" (1661) (OED, 1989, p. 619). The definition relating to forsaken religion is followed by a second, psychological, definition, "One who suffers from a perversion of the sexual instinct" (1892) (OED, 1989, p. 619). For present purposes, the definitions are of interest on three counts. First, the definition of sexual perversion is not given a prime position as the principal meaning of the term, but is superseded by non-sexual definitions. In my formulation non-sexual perversion is also given prominence. Second, the sexual definition places the pervert in the passive position of one who is afflicted by perversion. This fits with my assumption that perversion reverses early experiences of perceived victimisation. Third, his/her suffering is attributed to a perversion of instinct. This suggests innate determinants: I will be reinterpreting instinct in archetypal terms in Chapters Six and Seven.

In the same dictionary, Coverdale (1549) warns of the challenge in attempting to change perversity which, unlike other "frayleness" in man that may be "remedied by one or two warnings", "peruersitie is incurable and made worse by putting to of remedies" (1549) (OED, 1989, p. 619). According to this view, perversion is a condition so deeply ingrained that it would be unamenable to change through either punitive or therapeutic intervention, resonating with contemporary understanding of its addictive and compulsive nature.

The word perversion is listed in *Origins — A Short Etymological Dictionary of Modern English*, as deriving from the Latin *pervertere*, which is a composite of *vertere* "to turn" and *per* "thoroughly" (Partridge, 1958, p. 771). This definition might be regarded as emotionally and morally neutral in tone although it does suggest a deviation from the way that is "straight". Adair, citing Smith (1962), gives two associated meanings of *pervertere*: first, to "overturn, upset, overthrow, throw down", and second, "to subvert, put down, or confute" (Adair, 1993 p. 86). These definitions encompass the areas of both malevolent motivation and destructive behaviour. Adair also cites the Greek word στρεβλόω that was never adopted into English, which means both "pervert" and also means "twist or strain tight; or wrench a dislocated limb with a view to setting it; stretch on the wheel or rack, to rack, torture to extract evidence" (Adair, 1993, p. 86).

The *Bloomsbury Dictionary of Word Origins* places the Old English word *verse* within a large family of English words derived from the Latin verb *vertere*, or its past participle stem *vers*. *Verse*, means not only "turning" but also "turning of the plough" (Ayto, 1990, p. 557). Added to this earthy derivation is a metaphorical extension: the word "line" and the phrase "line of poetry" (1990, p. 557). *Vertere* itself comes from the Indo-European base *wert* which produced the English word *weird* (and suffix *ward*). According to the dictionary there is another negative connotation, in that *pervertere* can assume the meaning "to turn out badly" (1990, p. 557). In Old French and French the infinitive of the verb is *pervertir*, its orientation contrasting with the meaning of the verb *provertere*, "to turn forward" (1990, p. 577). Perversion now has a temporal quality, being associated with deviation from what might be regarded as healthy "forward looking" development. The idea of developmental failure is incorporated in my own formulation.

The *Cassell Dictionary of Word Histories* defines the verb "pervert", first used in the fourteenth to fifteenth centuries, as "to put to improper use" (Room, 1999, p. 455), whereas the derivative noun appears in the seventeenth century meaning, "a person who has been perverted" (1999, p. 455). The word pervert is generally used in a derogatory sense, often with partisan interest. The *Oxford English Dictionary* gives a theological definition for perversion as "change to error in religious belief" (OED, 1989, p. 619), contrasting with *conversion*, meaning changing to the correct religious belief. Applied in this manner, who is a pervert and who is not depends on one's point of view. The popular web-based encyclopaedia *Wikipedia* gives an illustration of this religious partiality in the attribution of perversion "in the pre-Vatican II era by some Roman Catholics to describe the process of converting from Roman Catholicism to Protestantism. Whereas a Protestant who joined Roman Catholicism was described as a *convert*, a Catholic who became a Protestant was called a *pervert*" (*Wikipedia*, 2006).

The religious connotation is broadened by Dollimore, a writer on sexual dissidence, who discusses biblical references to perversions. "In some of its numerous occurrences in the King James version the word is used quite generally, as more or less synonymous with sin, evil, or wickedness" (Dollimore, 1991, pp. 123–124). More specifically, it denotes wilful wrongness, the erring/error of men's ways, a transgression which is especially, rather than ordinarily, indicative of wickedness. In Acts 20:29–30 the perverse is even more clearly conceived as an inherent form of evil, a counterpart of external threat ("grievous wolves") and the more insidious for being an inner deviation: "For I know this, that after my departing shall grievous wolves enter in among you, not sparing the flock. Also of your own selves shall men arise, speaking perverse things, to draw away disciples after them" (Dollimore, 1991, p. 124).

Dollimore regards the Christian theory of evil as essentially implicated in how perversion is now conceptualised. He points to the eruption of evil in those closest to God, first the angels, and later man. The evil he describes is the perversion of "their most divine attribute, free will" (Dollimore, 1991, p. 124), and this then becomes the source of all evil. This turning or twisting (perversion) of free will signifies in the theoretical formulation of perversion in Chapter Seven.

Religious, moral, sexual, and psychological meanings have developed in parallel, largely subsumed under the same pejorative umbrella. As Laplanche and Pontalis point out, perversion could be "a very broad category" (Laplanche and Pontalis, 1973, p. 307). They cite Bardenat (1960), who refers to delinquency as a perversion of the moral sense, of prostitution as a perversion of the social instincts, and of eating disorders such as bulimia and dipsomania as perversion of the instinct of nutrition (Laplanche and Pontalis, 1973, p. 307). Perversion can link with what is inner, be it the will or the instinct, but is also given an "outer" meaning when applied in a social context, such as Bardenat's example of delinquency, which could be one example of the broader category of "deviance" that the sociologist Magill defines as "behaviour that violates some basic values and norms of society" (Magill, 1995, p. 226). He describes the relationship between deviance and social control from a conflict perspective, working from the propositions of, "the existence of an elite ruling class; the hegemonic power of that elite ruling class, resulting in inequity and inequality in the definitions of deviance; the creation of laws based on those definitions; and the differential application of those laws" (Magill, 1995, p. 227). Relevant to the use of the term "perversion", although not directly applied to the term, is one of the applications of the conflict perspective of deviance known as the labelling perspective, developed by Becker (1997):

> This describes a process by which both deviance and conformity are thought to be a result of people being defined (labelled) by others and then acting accordingly. More specifically, the labelling perspective takes into account the power of some individuals or groups to label others and have those labels "stick", while succeeding in deflecting negative labels themselves. (Magill, 1995, p. 227)

Although Magill is not discussing perversion directly, this echoes the previously cited religious use of perversion to denigrate and disempower through projection; a principal theme in my theoretical formulation of perversion. It is arguable that within a broader conceptual framework, perversion might more accurately be understood as deviance based on deception rather than sexual delinquency.

The sociologists Haralambos and Holborn (1995, pp. 387–390) present an overview of theories of deviance, dividing them into physiological, psychological, and functionalist. Psychological theories are depicted as regarding the deviant as different from the population as a whole, s/he is abnormal in the population and the abnormality predisposes him or her to deviance.

Psychological theories differ from physiological theories in that they see the deviant's sickness or abnormality as lying in the mind rather than the body. The functionalist perspective begins with society rather than the individual and does not look for the source of deviance in the biological or psychological nature of the individual. Functionalists emphasise the importance of shared norms and values and agree that, "social control mechanisms such as the police and the courts, are necessary to keep deviance in check and so protect social order" (Haralambos & Holborn, 1995, p. 389).

Considered in these terms, perversion could be understood as a physiological, psychological, or social category or as a relative category defined by its relationship to established or accepted norms which vary historically, geographically, and culturally. Alternatively, it might be seen as crossing the boundaries of all three perspectives.

Perversion is indeed a social offence subject to legal control within the bounds of the criminal justice system. The term is used in two ways in this context. The *Oxford Dictionary of Law* (Martin, 2003, pp. 365–366) defines the offence of "perverting the course of justice", as to "carry out an offence that tends or is intended to obstruct or defeat the administration of public justice" (Martin, 2003, p. 365). Common examples are given as "inventing false evidence to mislead a court (in either civil or criminal proceedings) or an arbitration tribunal, making false statements to the police, stealing or destroying evidence, threatening witnesses, and attempting to influence jurors" (Martin, 2003, pp. 365–366). Given the language used, it is relevant that the common-law offence of perverting the course of justice is described as, "overlapping with certain forms of *contempt* of court and with the separate offence of *tampering* with witnesses" (Martin, 2003, p. 366) (author's italics). As in perversion, the implication is that one party has "taken advantage" of another. Stone's *Justices' Manual* (Carr & Turner, 2005) supports this definition, quoting indictments and precedent in case law where perverse intention was sufficient for conviction. "The prosecution must prove either an intent to pervert the course of justice or an intent to do something which, if achieved, would pervert the course of justice" (Carr & Turner, 2005, p. 9025). The attribution of blame and accusation of contempt involve the questionable assumption that both criminality and perversion are conscious and controllable. The legal definitions also imply deceit through perversely seeking to ensure that the picture (evidence of the truth) is incomplete. In my formulation of perversion this external relational deception also occurs but has less conscious involvement, as it emanates intrapsychically from unconscious self-deception, with splits in the psyche militating against psychic integrity that would allow awareness of the whole picture.

The *Oxford Dictionary of Law* (Martin, 2003) defines another type of perversion within the legal system involving offence against the spirit rather than the letter of the law. A "perverse verdict" is the "verdict of a jury that is either entirely against the weight of the evidence or contrary to the judge's direction on a question of law" (Martin, 2003, p. 366). This, like perverse intent, assumes a wrongness in the mind that opposes what has been "rightly" instituted by those with power and authority.

This diverse usage of the concept of perversion forms the foundation upon which sexual pathology begins to settle, adopting some former meanings and rejecting others. The term "sexual" does not become firmly linked to "perversion" until the second half of the nineteenth century with the beginnings of contemporary psychiatric discourse. So by the 1990s Dollimore is able to describe the concept of sexual perversion as, "a modern notion, hardly more than a century old, [that] grew from medical discourses which were effectively displacing religious ones" (Dollimore, 1991, p. 144). He refers to early discussion of sexual morality guided by the teachings of the leading Christian Fathers, Augustine, Jerome, and Thomas Aquinas (Livingstone, 2000), promoting sex only for the purposes of procreation. All sexual practice that falls short of this requirement brings what is known as the "negative pleasure stigma" (Martins & Ceccarelli, 2003, p. 3). Foucault in his work on the history of sexuality, suggests that the nineteenth century middle-class institutionalised discussion between psychiatric specialists in sexual science actually creates "sexuality", a term that is still new in the nineteenth century when psychiatrists begin to participate in a longstanding discourse known as the "psychiatrization of perverse pleasure" (Foucault, 1979, p. 105). There is an implication that psychiatry legislates at the interface of morality and sexual behaviour. Martins and Ceccarelli (2003) describe how psychiatric discourse at this time is marked by a moralistic view, maintaining both theological and juridical positions. In so doing, the medical order usurps power from both church and court, claiming a privileged knowledge of perversion with authority to decide who else might have access to its domain. This attitude is exemplified by the marketing of the most prominent work in sexual psychopathology during this era, which, to avoid lay readership, is given the Latin title *Psychopathia Sexualis* and has a fly leaf specifying that sales of the book are: Strictly limited to members of the medical and legal profession, to teachers of and Post Graduate Students in the subject, educational institutions, libraries, book jobbers and book and not to the general public (Krafft-Ebing, [1886](1944)).

The author, Krafft-Ebing, a German physician and neurologist, is sequentially Professor of Psychiatry and Nervous Diseases at the Universities of Strasbourg (1872), Graz (1873), and Vienna (1889). He is recognised as an authority on deviant sexual behaviour and its medico-legal aspects. Being a methodical and detailed record keeper, *Psychopathia Sexualis* follows the taxonomic trend of his first major work, *Textbook of Insanity*. When he introduces the term perversion, he uses the heading "Paraesthesia of Sexual Feeling (Perversion of the Sexual Instinct)" (Krafft-Ebing, [1886]1944, p. 79), which he then defines as every expression of the sexual instinct "that does not correspond with the purpose of nature—i.e. propagation" ([1886]1944, p. 79). Although the title of his book indicates that it is only about sexuality, and Krafft-Ebing is remembered for his work in the sexual field, he also makes the interesting distinction between perversion, which he regards as a "disease" and perversity which he equates with "vice", adding that "one must investigate the whole personality of the individual and the original motive leading to the perverse act" ([1886]1944, pp. 79–80) in order to differentiate between the two. His main interest is in sexuality and he introduces and discusses the terms masochism, fetishism, and sadism. The hundreds of case studies that he records describe the sexual habits of a wide spectrum of men and women. His work forms a major part of creating a detailed inventory of deviant sexualities, by which he means sexual expressions in which the quest for procreation is subverted. To this nosography of deviant sexuality other psychiatrists add the categories homosexualism, voyeurism, and exhibitionism. Apart from usefully categorising sexual perversions, two points are of particular interest here. Krafft-Ebing recognises a possible wider use of the term perversion to include acts that are not sexually motivated (vice), although he seeks to distinguish between, rather than combine, the two. He also moves towards acknowledging a perverse psychic structure by stressing that perverse acts must be understood in the context of the whole personality.

As the psychiatric discourse on sexuality proceeds into the early twentieth century, the most prominent figures are Iwan Bloch (1872–1922), Magnus Hirschfeld (1868–1935), Havelock Ellis (1859–1939), and Sigmund Freud (1856–1939).

Bloch, a Berlin dermatologist, could be regarded as the first sexologist. He draws from fact and fiction in his understanding of perversion, studying the works of both Krafft-Ebing and Marquis de Sade, stating that "Marquis de Sade wrote in the form of a novel what Krafft-Ebbing did in his scientific work Psychopathia Sexualis a hundred years later" (Bloch, [1899]1948, p. 247). Bloch publishes *Marquis de Sade: his Life and Works* (Bloch, [1899]1948) and then discovers Marquis de Sade's manuscript of *The 120 Days of Sodom* (Bloch, [1904]1934), believed to be lost, and publishes it under the pseudonym Eugene Duhren. Bloch observes that in de Sade's novels only two characters show "an indication of an hereditary nature of sexual perversion" (Bloch, [1899]1948, p. 241) and he considers that most of the perverts described by de Sade "are products of their environment. Many of the libertines arrived at their diverse perverse sexual pursuits from experience and the desire for 'refinements' " (Bloch, [1899]1948, p. 240). In considering whether de Sade himself is insane, Bloch concludes "that de Sade was inflicted with a form of perversion", which he describes as "impulsive madness" (Bloch, [1899]1948, p. 245). This has been brought about by his experience of the French Revolution, spending "the formative years of his life, from 17 to 23, in the war, away from home and family . . . under the enormous moral corruption of the French army" (Bloch, [1899]1948, p. 246). Bloch seems to be saying that de Sade's "perversion" is not essentially *sexual*, but perhaps *social* and that he is impulsive and unstable due to lack of good containing relationships. Bloch thereby gives perversion a wider meaning, and continues to do so when he appears to accept Krafft-Ebing's assertion that "sadism and masochism are the main forms of psycho-sexual perversions" (Bloch, [1899]1948, p. 243) but then gives his own definition of sadism:

> Sadism is the purposely sought or accidentally presented connection of sexual excitation and pleasure with the actual or also only symbolic (ideal or illusory) occurrences of strange and terrifying events, destructive processes and actions, which threaten or destroy life, health and property of men or other living beings whereby the person receiving sexual pleasure from such events may be the originator or spectator, voluntary or involuntary. We believe that this definition covers all cases of sadism, *including word-sadism, torture, forms of rape, etc.* (Bloch, [1899]1948, pp. 244–245, author's italics)

This quotation clearly suggests that, for Bloch, perversion extends beyond generally accepted limits of sexuality and also that it can be represented symbolically within the psyche. Both observations accord with my own understanding of perversion.

Hirschfeld, a prominent German-Jewish physician, sexologist, and gay rights advocate, is both campaigner and scientist, investigating and cataloguing many varieties of sexuality, and emphasising the influence of early sexual experiences on future sexual development (Ellenberger, 1970, p. 778). He is interested in the study of a wide variety of sexual and erotic urges and is both quoted and caricatured in the press as a vociferous expert on sexual manners, receiving the epithet "the Einstein of Sex". He coins the term transvestism and aims to establish a non-prejudicial body of knowledge about men and women who cross-dress, which he publishes in 1910 as *The Transvestites: The Erotic Drive to Cross-Dress* (Hirschfeld, [1910]1991). Perhaps it is Hirschfeld's own trans-vestism and opposition to sexual prejudice which leads him to challenge the limited scope in the use of the term perversion. His suggestion that narcissism is also a sexual perversion involving a splitting of ideas is interesting because, in pulling narcissism into the category of perversion, he also extends the concept of perversion to cover narcissistic psychopathology (Hirschfeld, [1911]1947, p. 121), an area which, despite possible "intrapsychic eroticism", has no necessary associations to sexual behaviour. Despite his main sexual focus, like Krafft-Ebing and Bloch, he also suggests a non-sexual use of the term perversion. At the same time he reduces the scope of the term sexual perversion, criticising psycho-analysts for including transvestism as a perversion. He deduces that Krafft-Ebing would regard transvestites as either "sadistic women" and "masochistic men" suffering from "abuses of the instincts that are rooted in the sex drive" (Hirschfeld, [1910]1991, pp. 221–222). In Hirschfeld's view, this is only one of several categories of transvestism. He places most transvestites in the domain of "sexual intermediaries" (Hirschfeld, [1910]1991, p. 222) rather than perverts. In other words, he attempts to change the shape of the concept of perver-sion by increasing it to include narcissism while excluding a category to which he himself belongs, possibly because he understands that his own transvestism is associated more with sexual orientation than with feelings of vengeful attack.

Ellis's *Studies in the Psychology of Sex: Sexual Inversion* (1906) is one of the first scientific books not to treat homosexuality as a pathologi-cal condition. In another publication he also questions the use of the term perversion:

All these infantile forms of the sexual impulse—homosexual, scato-
logic, flagellatory, or what not—we are accustomed in our solemn
adult way to call "perversions". I have always preferred to call them
symbolisms, more or less auto-erotic in origin. (Ellis, 1919, p. 415)

He regards such symbolisms as natural, associating them with "a
normal and necessary play instinct" (1919, p. 415). Ellis does not
follow Hirschfeld in classifying narcissism as a perversion per se, but
does regard it as an extreme form of auto-eroticism which "might
become [a perversion] when deliberately pursued at the expense of
the normal objects of sexual attraction" (Ellis, 1927, p. 142).

With the weight of such eminent researchers joining the psychiatric discourse on perversion, the primacy of medical authority
is established and, as Dollimore states from a twentieth century
perspective, "sexual deviation comes to be understood as an illness or
a congenital abnormality rather than a sin" (Dollimore, 1991, p. 144).
While acknowledging this apparent shift, Dollimore highlights the
continuing significance of earlier understandings of perversion, maintaining that, "structures developed within the concept of the sinfully
perverse persist into modern theories of the sexually perverse" (1991,
p. 144).

This chapter has considered epistemological, moral, religious, judi-
cial, and sociological perspectives on perversion, and described the
narrowing of focus over time to the confines of medical and psychiatric
discourse which, although continuing some of the threads of earlier,
broader meanings, has primarily attended to the categorisation and
recording of sexual anomalies. The next chapter will see further prun-
ing of the concept of perversion as it is located more solidly within the
area of sexuality, this being one of the central themes of psycho-
analysis. Before moving on to this development, it is appropriate to
look back at two ranges of the non-sexual meaning of perversion that
begin to be lost as the concept enters medical and psychiatric
discourse. The first is definitions emphasising "turning", "turning
away", "overturning" (Partridge, 1958, p. 771) and the perversion of
free will (Dollimore, 1991, p. 124). This theme will be referred to again
in Chapter Seven in relation to the psychic turning away from healthy
development, from individuation, and "turning to" a subcentre in the
psyche representing perverse relationship, not necessarily of a sexual
nature. A second range, with a largely non-sexual theme, concerns

malevolence linked to destructive behaviour, "to subvert", "put down", "to confute" (Adair, 1993, p. 86) or put to improper use by exerting undue influence (Martin, 2003, pp. 365–366). All three biographies used to illustrate the theoretical formulation in Chapter Seven demonstrate these qualities, as they present in both sexual and non-sexual perversion.

It is generally agreed that sexual perversion is one among many forms of sexual expression, but it can also be argued that sexual perversion is one of a range of expressions of perversion. There is now evidence that some of the classical sexologists of the nineteenth and early twentieth century could understand perversion in this broader sense, although these views are largely washed aside by the sexual mainstream.

CHAPTER FOUR

From perversion to perverse structure

Not in madness but mad in craft

Shakespeare, *Hamlet*, Act 3: Scene 4

B y the beginning of the twentieth century, the first explorations into psychoanalytic theory and practice start to change the nature of sexual discourse amongst prominent psychiatrists. According to Homans, psycho-analysis breaks away "from the religious, political, and scientific authorities" of the past, and creates "a whole new form of thought and life" (Homans, 1989, p. xii). The swelling tide of interest in research and understanding of the range of human sexual expression and sexual choice, including perversion, now moves towards exploration of the possible role of contributory predispositional and unconscious motivational factors. This development leads Laplanche and Pontalis to observe that, "The most shocking thing about psycho-analysis is less its emphasis on sexuality than its introduction of unconscious phantasy into the theory of the mental functioning" (Laplanche & Pontalis, 1973, p. vii).

The recognition that psychic events are related to specific causes begins a shift from the medical model of diagnosis, classification, and recording of symptoms, to consideration of psychic structure and its relationship to psychopathology, with verification through focused studies of individuals and their personalities. Within psycho-analysis, perversion becomes identified through particular paradigms and characteristics, mainly concerning unconscious processes that combine to constitute the theory of a perverse psychic structure. The idea of psychic structure challenges the notion of a simple link between isolated symptoms and diagnosis, not only in the case of perversion, but also for neurosis and psychosis, as perverse, neurotic, and psychotic structures begin to be distinguished.

From this time onwards theorists address the concept of perversion in relation to psychic structure as a whole. For example, Filippini (2005, p. 762) places perversion for diagnostic purposes on a spatial map of psychopathology, with a continuum ranging from narcissistic disorder to borderline disorder, and further to malignant narcissism, and finally to the most extreme forms of antisocial personality disorder. This axis is crossed by the axis of perversion. Around the intersection of the two axes is an area of varying density that represents the range of types of behaviour which can be defined either as narcissistic perversion, or as relational perversion. From the opposite perspective, Kernberg (2006) identifies perversion through its exclusion of the normal psychic structure and associated normal sexuality which achieves:

> the integration of early, pregenital fantasy and activity with genital fantasy and activity, the capacity to, achieve sexual excitement and orgasm in intercourse, and the capacity to integrate into sexual fantasy, play, and activity aspects of the sadistic, masochistic, voyeuristic, exhibitionistic, and fetishistic components of polymorphous perverse infantile sexuality. (Kernberg, 2006, p. 21)

Other approaches are those of: (a) Coen (1992, p. 227) who has a conflict model that places diagnostic focus on the complex multiple functions served by sexually perverse behaviour which can be adaptive, reparative, defensive, or gratifying: (b) Khan (1979, pp. 120–121), who includes the other in his three basic features of sexual perversions: the necessity of the presence and compliance of an external object; the nature and quality of an organised phantasy-system, unconscious and unknowable; and the reality of an experiential situation in which space motility, sight, and touch are essential ingredients: and (c) Goldberg (2006, pp. 41–45), who also makes a threefold diagnosis, based on the existence of first, sexualisation (representing for him a lack of structure and the avoidance of a painful affective state); second, vertical splitting (also indicating the need for structural repair); and third the individual dynamics of the patient, in which he is particularly concerned with Oedipal and pre-Oedipal problems. He views psychic structure as "a broad set of capacities or enduring functions" (2006, p. 41) but he links perversion to *structural deficit* requiring psychotherapeutic re-establishment of structure through focussing on desexualisation.

Kernberg identifies *containment* of would-be perverse qualities as the key difference between perversion and normality, and of critical significance in the evolving psychoanalytic literature that divides sexual perversions into two major groups according to the level of severity (2006, p. 22–24). He considers that, "An important common feature of perverse scenarios at the higher or less severe level is the containment of aggression" (2006, p. 22) within the bounds of love and eroticism. The more severely pathological level or organisation of perversion, typically found in patients with borderline personality organisation, is characterised by Oedipal conflicts condensed with severe pre-Oedipal conflicts accompanied by dominant aggression. He classifies the pathology of perversion from a psychostructuralist viewpoint into six major groups from least to most severe: in the context of the neurotic personality organisation; at the level of borderline personality organisation; combined with narcissistic personality disorder; in cases of malignant narcissism; in antisocial personality disorder; and as part of a psychotic personality organisation.

As the concept of perversion moves from medical and psychiatric discourse into the domain of psycho-analysis, it becomes securely wedded to the concept of sexuality. The identification of specific qualities within this conceptual marriage, qualities of the perverse psychic structure as understood by a range of theorists beginning with Freud, are elucidated thematically in the remainder of this chapter. These qualities, plus psycho-analytic offshoots from the core theoretical stance, are then summarised in the following chapter and offered as support for expanding the concept of perversion beyond the traditional boundaries of sexuality, giving a broader conceptual framework that includes both sexual and non-sexual perversion.

The section below includes post-Freudian interpretations, theoretical revisions, and criticism from outside the analytic domain.

Jungian and post-Jungian thought and ideas are largely excluded so that these can be addressed in Chapter Six, which focuses on concepts from analytical psychology that contribute to the theoretical formulation of perversion in Chapter Seven.

Sexual perversion

Freud accepts perversion as a debasement of adult sexual relationship. In describing perverse forms of intercourse, he states, "These activities cannot . . . be regarded as being . . . harmless . . . in love-relationships. They are ethically objectionable, for they degrade the relationships of love between two human beings from a serious matter to a convenient game, attended by no risk and no spiritual participation" (Freud, 1908d, p. 200). However, sexually perverse activity in infancy does not have this derogatory tag.

Psychosexual development

Less than fifty years since perversion is first studied scientifically, Freud becomes a major contributor to the debate with the publication of his *Three Essays on the Theory of Sexuality* (Freud, 1905d) which, through case studies of psycho-analytic treatment, link perversion with the development of the sexual instinct in human beings from infancy to maturity.

Freud divides early sexual development into oral, anal, and phallic phases, corresponding to erotogenic zones of the body, and culminating in the desire for the opposite-sex parent, and removal of the parent of the same sex. At all stages there is a conflict between the need for expression of instinctual sexual drives and both external and intrapsychic factors that may block such expression. In the critical phallic, or Oedipal, phase there is inevitable conflict between sexual desire and fear of retribution from the opposite-sex parent. Conflict is dealt with by banishing instinctual (sexual and aggressive) drives from consciousness by means of defences such as repression, denial, rationalisation, reaction formation, and projection. Through repression and sublimation, polymorphous sexuality is channelled into genital heterosexuality. Whereas neurotic symptoms represent a defence against infantile or perverse sexual drives, people who react to sexual frustrations with regression toward infantile sexuality are classified as perverts.

Sexual perversion in adulthood

Freud conceives of the sexual drive as having a source, an aim, and an object. He emphasises the aim of genital heterosexuality as the constant and defining factor in normal sexuality. Perversion rejects the normal aim and object and "ousts them completely" (Freud, 1905d, p. 161), resulting in behaviour that deviates from the normal sexual aim, or fixates on a sexual object other than a mature member of the opposite sex. For Freud perversions are, in essence, "sexual activities which either (a) extend, in an anatomical sense, beyond the regions of the body that are designed for sexual union, or (b) linger over the immediate relations to the sexual object which should normally be traversed rapidly on the path towards the final sexual aim" (Freud, 1905d, p. 165). Freud makes it clear that perversion does not violate biological laws. One does not become a pervert, but may remain one if psychic conflict obstructs normal development. Perversion can be understood as "the persistence into adult life of elements of infantile 'polymorph-perverse' sexual activity at the expense of adult genitality. These infantile strivings have failed to undergo the normal transformations of puberty, and have failed also to succumb to the defence mechanisms that would have converted them into neurotic symptoms" (Gillespie, 1956, p. 396). As such, they would have remained unconscious: "in neurosis the repressed phantasy breaks through only as an egodystonic symptom, . . . in perversion it remains capable of consciousness, being egosyntonic and pleasurable . . ." (1956, p. 397).

Fetishism as a model of perversion

Freud (1927e, p. 154) contends that in every category of sexual perversion there is the belief in the woman with a penis, or phallic woman, but fetishism is the category most often presented as prototypical of perversion. Through a combination of castration anxiety and contradictory beliefs in the reality of the mother's penis (disavowal) (Freud, 1927e, p. 153), the fetishistic object, representing the missing penis of the mother, is the detail that stands for the whole. The diagnostic criterion for fetishism is that the fetishistic object must be a necessary and sufficient condition for sexual gratification. In other words, the object must have moved from a representation of the loved mother object to being a replacement for her. Although fetishism is the prototype, Freud describes a number of other sexual perversions: voyeurism (looking at others naked or having sex) and its counterpart exhibitionism (displaying the genitals); sadism and masochism, another pair of opposites, (the infliction of pain or humiliation or the wish to be subjected to this); bestiality (sex with animals); pederasty (sex with children); and transvestism (cross-dressing). All have some form of "unsuitable substitute for the sexual object" (Freud, 1905d, pp. 136–153) thereby fitting the prototype of fetishism, as well as complying with Freud's definition of perversion in the previous paragraph.

Characteristics of sexual perversion

Perversion as a defence

Freud's own views on perversion evolve after *Three Essays on the Theory of Sexuality* (1905d) and by the time he writes "A child is being beaten" (1919e) he has moved from seeing perversions simply as residues of the pregenital component drives that have neither been sublimated nor transformed into neurotic symptoms, to understanding the beating fantasy as defensive. Fixation on the fantasy of another child (oneself) being beaten by a teacher (parent) protects the child from Oedipal conflicts. Freud then attaches a defensive function to perversions more generally. Gillespie (1956, p. 398) agrees with Freud's interpretation of this case, that the perverse defence is against guilt as well as anxiety, and Verhaeghe (2004, pp. 127–128) contrasts this denial of guilt, typical of the pervert, with the neurotic's tendency to overtly display his guilt.

Despite wide acceptance of the defensive nature of the perverse structure, there is less agreement about what is being defended against. Freud's explanation is that the defence is against "castration anxiety aroused by oedipal wishes and also attacks from the superego with its oedipal origins" (Parsons, 2000, p. 43). Mawson describes "an organised system of defences against, for example, psychotic disintegration, primitive confusion and helplessness" (Mawson, 1999, p. 1), whereas Steiner (1993, pp. 10–11) envisages a psychic retreat that protects the patient from both paranoid–schizoid and depressive anxieties and can become a semi-permanent residence (1993, pp. 1–2) where relief from anxiety is provided, albeit at the cost of isolation, stagnation, and withdrawal.

Narcissism

There is a difference between a perverse psychic structure leading to sexually perverse behaviour, and personality traits present in conditions such as narcissism, which might display only some sexually perverse tendencies. Likewise, narcissistic traits can be found within the perverse psychic structure. Freud, however, closely links narcissism and perversion—sexual perversion being one of a number of disorders in which the body is used as a sexual object (Freud, 1914c, p. 73). This connection is supported by Meltzer (1979, pp. 132–133) who understands sexual perversion as developing from a narcissistic personality disorder in which good objects are devalued and depreciated, and by Steiner (1993, p. 6), who describes narcissistic object relationships in perversion based on projective identification, when part of the self is denied and projected into the object. This leads to confusion between the self and the object and between the symbol and the thing symbolised. "... concrete thinking ... arises when symbolisation is interfered with [leading] to an increase in anxiety and in rigidity" (Steiner, 1993, p. 27). Steiner describes how narcissism and sexual perversion can be linked in an intrapsychic relationship when a dominant "narcissistic part of the personality can acquire a disproportionate power by gaining a hold on the healthier part of the personality" creating a "perverse liaison" (Steiner, 1982, p. 250). In this way compliance is obtained from what Joseph (1975, p. 205) refers to as a pseudo-cooperative part of the self. Steiner stresses the importance of assessing how the destructive part is dealt with by the rest of the personality, whether it is taken over by, or opposes, its oppressor.

Kernberg (1990, pp. 325–326) distinguishes the effects of narcissism from those of the borderline personality in sexual perversion. In the narcissistic personality structure the perverse scenario is infiltrated by aggressive aspects of condensed Oedipal and pre-Oedipal conflicts. The most dangerous outcome is malignant narcissism, into which the aggressive drive derivatives are integrated into the grandiose pathological self.

Rosenfeld (1971) and Fillipini (2005) both link sexual perversion to narcissism. Fillipini (2005, pp. 760–761) describes how the narcissist relates to self-objects, using the other only as a mirror to verify his own identity and support his self-esteem, creating an unequal power relationship. Although sexual perversion is more organised than narcissism, Riesenberg Malcolm (1999, p. 1) notes that when narcissistic phenomena cannot be transformed sufficiently, they can give rise to different pathological syndromes among which are the sexual perversions.

Rigidity

Characteristic of the perverse structure is a rigidity of thought, feeling, and action, all intricately combined with a number of defence mechanisms.

Several authors stress the rigidity of the psychic structure behind sexual perversion and its characteristic of being unaltered by experience. Verhaeghe (2004, p. 405) gives the diagnostic criterion for perversion as the enactment in reality of a rigid pregenital scenario that compulsively imposes itself on the pervert and establishes a relationship of power. For Steiner (1993, p. 27), rigidity in sexual perversion results when a projected part of the self cannot be withdrawn from objects and returned to the ego. This requires facing reality so that mourning can proceed. If projections are not withdrawn, the only way of retaining contact with lost parts of the self is through a possessive hold on the objects that have been projected. Coen (1992, p. 224) contrasts the pervert's rigidity with the neurotic's relatively good ability to express conflict in fantasy and to handle it in his mind. McDougall (1972, p. 371) distinguishes between fantasies or activities that might appear sexually perverse but are actually part of a normal sexual relationship, and those that have this quality of rigidity and demand for narrow compliance characterising sexual perversion. Kaplan also identifies a "quality of desperation and fixity" (Kaplan, 1991, p. 10) in sexual perversion comparing it with the perceived experience of choice in "kinky" sex. The perverse psychic structure leads to a singularly impoverished fantasy life that has little erotic freedom and is "fundamentally compulsive" (McDougall, 1972, p. 371). Far from being exploratory, there is only one way of achieving sexual pleasure. McDougall compares the perverse scenario to a children's game, as if it were an invented sexuality but lacking in playfulness because of the child's desperation both to avoid recognising the genital relation between the parents and also to avoid castration anxiety:

> Whether this be the script of the sadomasochist with his concentration on pain often aimed directly at his genitals or those of his partner, or the fetishist who reduces the game of castration to beaten buttocks and bodily constriction (the important bodily marks which symbolize castration but are so readily effaced) or the transvestite who makes his own genitals vanish while he infiltrates himself into his mother's garments in order to take on her identity . . .. In every instance the plot is the same: castration does not hurt and in fact is the very condition of erotic pleasure. (McDougall, 1972, p. 378)

The sexual game has rigid rules and employs the defence mechanisms of disavowal and negation, splitting and projection, regression and manic defence (1972, p. 373). It not only lacks playfulness but is a desperate attempt to ward off rage and murderous or suicidal impulses, making use of "reversals, displacements and symbolic equivalents" (1972, p. 377). Using her less emotive term, "neosexualities", to describe perversions, she stresses that "the leading theme of the neosexual plot is invariably castration . . . the triumph of the neosexual scenario lies in the fact that the castrative aim is only playfully carried out . . . [Perversions] are all substitute acts of castration and thus serve to master castration anxiety in illusionary fashion, at every conceivable level" (McDougall, 1985, p. 253).

Denial

Ruth Stein describes the denial in perversion comprehensively as "a specific relational matrix, sexualized, paranoid, symbiotic, grandiose pact, an implicit contract signed against reality" (Ruth Stein, 2005, p. 793). Denial of the parents as a sexual couple threatens psychic growth, (Manninen & Absets, 2000, p. 197), which is further impeded or damaged if the child simultaneously loses the nurturing of parents through neglect or abuse. Perversion can be the child's attempt to compensate for a lack of confirmation of himself by the parents.

McDougall regards denial as a prime instigating factor for the establishment of a perverse psychic structure. "Through an infinity of symbolic displacements and cutting of certain associative links, sexual desire is furnished with new objects, new zones and new aims" (McDougall, 1972, p. 378). In particular (1972, p. 381) she suggests an unconscious collusion by the mother in denying, by denigration, the father's phallic function. Andre (2006, pp. 110–112), writing from a Lacanian perspective, supports this view, describing how the mother derides the father in her discourse with the child, designating the father in the Oedipal conflict as "a derisory personality" (2006, p. 111), a purely fictional character who himself disavows the status of the symbolic father as the depository of law and authority. Andre compares him to a leading actor who either never appears on the stage or has no script.

Chasseguet-Smirgel (1974, p. 349) also sees parental attitude (both mother and father) as decisive in either confirming or denying the boy's desire to be mother's partner at the expense of sexual truth. She understands perversion as a magical attempt to deny inevitable infantile traumas through the creation of an anal-sadistic universe (penis=faeces=child) in which difference of sex and difference between generations are denied: "differentiation from mother is unnecessary, father is nonexistent, pregenitality is idealized, and sublimation is impossible and unnecessary" (Chasseguet-Smirgel, 1985, p. 141). Since difference is abolished, so is reality, which demands an acknowledgment of separation and consequently of loss (1985, pp. 2–6). As Ogden states, "Not knowing deprives us of our sense of who we are and yet to know is to see that which we cannot bear to see" (Ogden, 1989, p. 3).

A number of theorists emphasise the use of denial as a defence against the acknowledgment of sexual difference. Kaplan describes the pervert as adopting a "mental strategy" (Kaplan, 1991, p. 9) by using a social stereotype of masculinity and femininity to deceive the onlooker about the unconscious meaning of his behaviour. McDougall (1972, p. 377–380) asserts that the sight of the female genital organs without the penis is terrifying to the boy, not only because it confirms the possibility of castration, but also because mother not having a penis impels the boy to recognise the role of the father's penis in the primal scene. Freud introduces the term "disavowal" (Freud, 1927e, p. 153) to mean the simultaneous denial and recognition of reality, particularly the reality of the female penis. At first he postulates a duality of belief, causing a split in the ego that could lead to the substitution of a fetishistic object for the female penis, but he later modifies the idea that the fetishist is able to hold two contradictory ideas about the maternal phallus, to a belief that due to lack of knowledge of the female genital the child suspends the decision about the mother's lack of a penis, leaving it uncertain: "all the various reactions . . . survive . . . including contradictory ones" (Freud, 1941f, p. 299). Bak (1968, p. 16), supporting this later position, associates the uncertainty about the nature of the female genital with the pervert's uncertainty about his own sexual identity. He thinks of perversions as acted out in various forms through identification with the phallic mother, with related objects, or by a narcissistic split through projection.

Rangell (1991, p. 17) also highlights the denial of sexual identity, arguing that an unconscious fantasy of feminine identification is the common foundation of all perversions in men. This negative Oedipal constellation, in which the father–son relationship is sado-masochistically perverted, is also described by Manninen and Absets (2000, p. 193). Fear of castration causes the boy to identify with the opposite, and offer himself to the father as the feminine or castrated object. This masochistic position is also a defence against the wish to rob the father of his sadistic phallus, and leads to an eroticised triumph as the terror of castration is defeated. Manninen and Absets (2000, p. 199) see this as the wish for sex with the mother transformed into a wish to have sex as the mother does, making the boy into a woman. McDougall (1972, p. 375) connects the resulting disturbance in sexual identity with compulsive perverse sexual behaviour, as the boy needs constant confirmation of his sexual identity.

Adair attributes this dynamic to an inability to move beyond disavowal or relinquish the delusion of the maternal phallus. The pervert remains in a state of denial, simultaneously holding two contradictory beliefs, inspiring "body" or "motor" hallucinations. The pervert "sadistically twists and wrenches the sexual machinery of the body" to conform to his hallucinated perception of reality (Adair, 1993, p. 88). McDougall (1972, p. 379) believes that he creates "a sexual mythology whose true meaning he no longer recognises". This perverse denial is distinguished by Anna Freud (1936, pp. 73–99) from playful denial in fantasy since it is associated with action. In perversion the unconscious motivation is hidden by action rather than by a psychological symptom.

Feldman, Bak, and Eidelber (1952, pp. 324–325) describe a particular kind of denial in perversion when the ego misleads the superego by presenting less objectionable polymorphous-perverse features and disguising the aim of genital orgasm directed towards an external object. Sperling (1956, p. 58) reports the opposite role of the superego in group perversions, where a leader, usually with a spontaneous perversion himself, takes over the role of the superego in a group, inducing the adoption of perversions by other group members, who deny connection with their own superegos.

Splitting and idealisation

The defence mechanisms of splitting and idealisation work together in the dynamics of perversion. Freud (1914c, p. 70) introduces the concept of the ego ideal into psychoanalytic theory, as a development of the concept of primary narcissism. He describes the inability to relinquish satisfactions once enjoyed leading to a narcissistic idealisation of the fantasised perfection of childhood. There is a failure of the normal operation of the ego-ideal, with the father no longer a model for his son (Freud, 1914c, p. 91). The mother simultaneously denigrates the father so he is no longer envied by the son, while acting seductively towards him herself. This dynamic is described by McDougall (1972, p. 378) in connection with denial. She (1972, p. 374) also describes how the mother becomes idealised while the father has a negative role in the pervert's inner object world. If the mother colludes and allows the boy to usurp the father's position and no longer identify with him, this distortion in the ego-ideal is accompanied by a correlative distortion of reality (Chasseguet-Smirgel, 1974). The "mother fosters an illusion in making the son believe that, with his infantile sexuality, he is a perfect partner for her, and therefore has nothing to envy in his father, thus arresting his development. His ego-ideal, instead of directing itself towards the genital father and his penis, remains henceforth attached to a pregenital model" (1974, p. 349). She is describing the son's idealisation of his pregenital self as part of a parent–child sexual couple, by which the father is displaced.

Chasseguet-Smirgel actually characterises perversion by a "compulsion to idealise" (Chasseguet-Smirgel, 1989, p. 90), particularly the idealisation of the "objects, erotogenic zones and instincts of the anal phase" (1989, p. 89), in order for the anal-sadistic aggression in perversion to be ego-syntonic and thereby avoid repression. Gillespie (1956) describes the part that the ego plays in this anal-sadistic defensive manoeuvre by adopting a certain piece of infantile sexuality that enables it to "ward off the rest" (1956, p. 402). This is achieved outside the normal constraints of reality; by "a split in the ego and in the object such that an idealized object and a relatively anxiety-free and guilt-free part-ego are available for the purposes of a sexual relationship" (1956, p. 402).

Aggression and sadism

Like Freud, Gillespie (1940), Greenacre (1996), and Chasseguet-Smirgel (1985) all regard sadism as central to perversion. Chasseguet-Smirgel (1978, p. 28) identifies the quality of regression in perversion as anal-sadistic. Mawson refers to the erotic pleasure and triumph generated by perverse cruelty (Mawson, 1999, pp. 1 & 7) and Parsons observes how "Sadism and masochism have the characteristic of engaging the object in an intense relationship but on the uncompromising condition that intimacy and union are never present" (Parsons, 2000, p. 43). Kernberg (1988, p. 1007) considers aggression to be a normal ingredient of infantile sexuality, love relations, and sexual excitement, but developed harmfully in perversion. The dependent child is unable to show aggression towards the mother so the aggression becomes libidinised into sadism and is directed towards others whom the pervert seeks to control, as he himself feels controlled. Libidinisation, combined with idealisation, offers a defence against both aggression and paranoid anxieties. In Glover's view this makes perversion not just the negative of neurosis but also of certain forms of psychosis (Glover, 1933, p. 496).

Glasser (1979, p. 281;1998, p. 888) compares aggression and sadism in relationships, distinguishing two types of defensive manoeuvres that can occur in perversion. The first is protection of the psyche by eliminating the dangerous other; the second is preservation of the other, making him suffer. Both incorporate a violent or potentially violent response to the other. Freud (1924c), Rosenfeld (1971), and Klein (1975) all link the sadistic option in perversion to the death instinct. Stoller (1977, pp. 96–110) makes a similar distinction between hostility and aggression. He sees perversion as the erotic form of hatred, and perverse acts as motivated by hostility rather than just aggression. The pervert wishes to harm the object, and hostility is demonstrated in the fantasy of revenge for trauma or humiliation in childhood, converting these experiences into triumph. Hatred expressed through sexual action is seen as an integral part of perversion and is a necessary component to comply with his definition. "Perverse people . . . deal with their partners as if the others were not real people but rather puppets to be manipulated on the stage where the perversion is played" (1977, p. 105). He presents two hypotheses: (a) that trauma or frustration of childhood is aimed precisely at the sexual anatomical apparatus and its functions or at the child's masculinity or femininity, and (b) that sexual excitement is most likely to be set off at the moment when adult reality resembles the childhood trauma or frustration (1977, p. 105). Mawson supports Stoller's view in referring to "the erotic pleasure and triumph generated by perverse cruelty" (Mawson, 1999), but Cooper (1991, pp. 23–34) reverses the argument suggesting that the hostility that Stoller (1991) correctly identifies as at the core of perversion is used as "an aid to the maintenance of dehumanization" (Cooper, 1991, p. 24) and is actually not the cause of the dehumanisation. His argument, however, does not always distinguish between perverse fantasies and perverse acts or between magical illusions and delusions.

Meltzer describes an analogous intrapsychic destructiveness, with the influence of harmful parts of the personality replacing dependence on good objects with a passivity towards bad parts of the self (Meltzer, 1979, p. 132). Rosenfeld (1971, pp. 174–175) also discusses perverse interaction in the form of violent attacks between different parts of the self, and Steiner describes how a healthy part of the self colludes with a "narcissistic gang" (Steiner, 1993, p. 104) and allows itself to be taken over.

Addiction and Compulsion

Perversion is repetitive and compulsive. Kaplan describes it as "a central preoccupation of the person's existence" that "demands performance" (Kaplan, 1991, p. 10), Money refers to "paraphilic addiction" (Money, 1988, p. 148), Mawson to "perverse addiction" (Mawson, 1999, p. 6), and McDougall, who associates the urgency and compulsivity of perversion with a manic defence against depressive guilt, describes how:

> The eternal quest for the father, for something which stands between the child and the omnipotent mother, contributes to the compulsive character of perverse sexuality ... That which is missing in the internal world is sought in an external object or situation, for there is a vital lack or blank in the ego structure of the pervert, and this in turn is due to a failure in symbolism. This failure concerns the meaning of the primal scene, and the role of the father's penis. (McDougall, 1972, p. 375)

Steiner's theory of psychic retreats (Steiner, 1993, p. 103–104) explains the compulsion of sexual perversion in terms of intrapsychic coercion within the patient's pathological organisation, an organisation within which, due to feelings of dependency, he remains or frequently returns "for protection to avoid catastrophe" (1993, p. 103). He is compulsively driven because he "remains stuck in the organisation even though the conditions which led to his original dependence on it no longer exist" (1993, p. 103).

Adler writes of a complementary relationship between this addictive, compulsive dynamic and the sublimation Freud regarded as necessary in the move towards genital sexuality. Sublimation he sees as "transcended addiction" (Adler, 1986, p. 187) and addiction as "either lapsed or an aborted sublimation" (1986, p. 187). He refers to well known "addict authors" (1986, p. 187) who demonstrate an oscillation between the two states, suggesting "an alternation or concurrence of creativity and addictive behaviours" (1986, p. 188). Adler construes both sublimation and addiction as having recourse to transitional objects as they seek "a bridge to the other" (1986, p. 189), the first internally and the second externally. "Failure to achieve a successful transition from the infant's symbiotic state, to attain adequate constancy, separation, and individuation, locks the individual into perseverative and oscillating behaviour" (1986, p. 189).

CHAPTER FIVE

Relationship between the perverse structure and non-sexual perversion

That one may smile and smile and be a villain

Shakespeare, *Hamlet*, Act 1: Scene 5

Non-sexual perversion

There is little direct theoretical focus on non-sexual perversion which, if attended to at all, is treated as a fringe extension to sexual perversion. Although Laplanche and Pontalis, in defining the terminology of psycho-analysis, privilege *sexual* perversion, they also add that, "Before Freud's time the term was used, as indeed it still is, to denote 'deviations' of instinct (in the traditional sense of predetermined behaviour characteristic of a particular species and comparatively invariable as regards its performance and its object)" (Laplanche & Pontalis, 1973, pp. 306–307). This leads them to consider perversion as "a very broad category" (1973, p. 307) and to posit "a multitude of forms" (1973, p. 307) such as "perversions of the 'moral sense' (delinquency), of the 'social instincts' (prostitution), and of the instinct of nutrition (bulimia, dipsomania)" (1973, p. 307). They also associate cruelty and malevolence in character or behaviour with perversion.

Ruth Stein (2005, p. 781) identifies a gradual transition from the narrowly defined concept of sexual perversion to a wider understanding that includes character perversion, perversion in organisations, in relationships, and in the therapeutic transference. She (2005, p. 776) considers that non-sexual behaviour emanating from a perverse state of mind might equally well be described as perversion. Caper (1998, p. 545) states that perversion can now be redefined in terms of unconscious object relationship, and Meltzer (1979, p. 134) believes that perversion can be expressed through any mode of relationship and that there is no human activity that cannot be perverted, since "the essence of the perverse impulse is to alter good into bad while preserving the appearance of good" (1979, p. 132).

The Oedipus complex

Some critics of the narrower view of perversion take the Oedipus complex as their focal point since it is a cornerstone of psycho-analytic theory. From a non-analytic perspective, Dollimore (1991, pp. 203 & 195) criticises the normative deployment of the Oedipus complex for being "Essentially . . . a theory of how the human being becomes positioned within the existing system of social and sexual difference as a result of a critical and fraught relationship with his or her parents" (1991, p. 195). In other words, he is criticising an exclusively sexual interpretation of infantile conflicts. Manninen and Absets (2000, pp. 193–194) partially accommodate this criticism by broadening their understanding of castration anxiety to include Oedipal and pre-Oedipal anxiety rather than exclusively sexual conflicts. They stress the threat of helplessness and the fear of destruction at the roots of castration anxiety; a theme adopted by Glasser (1979) within the core complex of perversion. He describes the push–pull of two opposing dynamics; "a deep-seated and pervasive longing for an intense and most intimate closeness to another person, amounting to a 'merging', a 'state of one', a 'blissful union' " (1979, p. 278), opposed by a fear that such longings will lead to a permanent loss of a separate self and of being engulfed or annihilated by the object.

Fairbairn (1944) also gives a non-sexual meaning to Oedipal issues, attributing them to conflict between need for each of the parents and fear of rejection by one of them.

> The child finds it intolerable enough to be called upon to deal with a single ambivalent object; but when he is called upon to deal with two, he finds it still more intolerable. He, therefore, seeks to simplify a complex situation, in which he finds himself confronted with two needed objects, by converting it into one in which he will only be confronted with a single needed object and a single rejecting object; and he achieves this aim, with, of course, a varying measure of success, by concentrating upon the needed aspect of one parent and the rejecting aspect of the other. He thus, for all practical purposes, comes to equate one parental object with the needed object, and the other with the rejecting object; and by so doing *the child constitutes the Oedipus situation for himself.* (Fairbairn, 1944, p. 89)

The concept of position

Parsons (2000) challenges the sequential arrangement of Freud's stages of psycho-sexual development, substituting Klein's concept of position. He is valuing not the actual position, but the concept of position itself, which he defines as:

> a constellation of impulses, fantasies, anxieties, defences and object relationships, which has a particular quality deriving from the point in development at which it arises, but without a definitive endpoint at which it disappears. Instead it remains present, latent or active, allowing that aspect of a person's internal world to go on evolving throughout the whole of life. This makes it possible to conceptualise developmental processes in a more mobile, open-ended way than was available before. (Parsons, 2000, p. 40)

He makes the point that the reworking of "developmental stage" into "position" opens up new ways of thinking about maturity, including the understanding of personality development as a lifelong process. A position or "underlying constellation" (Parsons, 2000, p. 41) can be revisited and does not require development to be a linear process.

Traits

Arlow theorises that a perversion or tendency towards perversion can be "replaced in later life by an abnormal character trait" (Arlow, 1991, p. 63). He suggests that such traits "are genetically related to the sexual perversions in that structurally they are reproductions in exquisite detail of the defensive mechanisms that characterize some specific perversion" (1991, p. 63). He gives the example of "unrealistic characters" (1991, p. 63), patients who defensively "look away" (1991, p. 63) from unpleasant or threatening reality, which he associates with their earlier voyeuristic and fetishistic interests or practices. A variation of this group are "petty liars" (1991, p. 64) who prevent others from seeing the truth in order to avoid being confronted with the truth themselves. A third type is "the practical joker or hoaxer" (1991, p. 65) who instils panic or anxiety in others, that gratifies his aggressive needs as well as giving a sense of power that culminates in exposing the hoax.

Meltzer (1979, p. 134) suggests that the adjective "perverse" should relate to the impulse, as in perverse sexuality, and the noun "perversion" should refer to an organised perverse structure, not just to sexual perversion. He then categorises all types of perversion according to three levels of severity, "*habitual, addicted and criminal*" (1979, p. 134). Habitual perversion is the least severe since it "can be attuned to the exigencies of external relationships. Despite this, it contains all the characteristics of an addictive, narcissistic organisation:

> the attack on the truth, the dismantling of the object to form the fetishistic plaything, the autoerotic sensuality, the defence against depressive pain, the alteration of the relationship to pain into masochism by tricks of projective identification with the victim of sadistic phantasy. (Meltzer, 1979, p. 134)

At the next level of severity, the perversion has become addictive and is accompanied by a "mood of despair" and a "suicidal impulsivity" (1979, p. 134). For Meltzer, criminal perversions, often associated with violence, are the most severe. "This is in essence psychopathy, a category of psychosis in which intellectual judgement is unimpaired and moral judgement non-existent" (1979, p. 135).

Perverse thought

Several theorists refer to types of cognitive perversion, described as "perverse thinking" or "perverse thought". Ermann describes perverse thinking as bound to neither aggressive nor sexual experience but a functional mental state outside reality and fantasy. "It occurs whenever an individual gets into an existential irritation [such as the child's observation of the absence of a penis in the female] which demands a fundamental change" (Ermann, 2005, p. 188). He believes that perverse thinking, based on denial, is associated for some individuals with the defensive "psychic retreat" described by Steiner (1993). Perverse denial contrasts with neurotic denial in that it does not change reality, "but it creates another reality besides the objective one" (Ermann, 2005, p. 189).

Although he does not use the term "perversion" or even the adjective "perverse", Money-Kyrle (1968, pp. 692–693) also describes perverse distortions in cognition. He makes an analogy with Freud's two principles of mental functioning (Freud, 1911b) in which the infant is described as failing to recognise what is intolerable to him, a mechanism familiar in disavowal. Money-Kyrle regards recognition as the basic act in cognitive development and, "When a concept is not available to complete an act of recognition, its place is usually taken by a misconception" (1968, p. 693). In other words, there is a perversion of truth. Waddell and Williams (1991, pp. 203–213) also describe the functioning of a destructive part of the self devoted to distortion and attacks on truth.

Sánchez-Medina describes perverse thought as "a special type of thought disorder" (Sánchez-Medina, 2002, p. 1345), a hypothesis based on Bion's work on the psychotic and non-psychotic parts of the personality. He describes perverse thought as "an attack on the knowledge process, and therefore truth" (2002, p. 1345), and argues that "the perverse" could be regarded as "an intermediary alternative between psychosis and non-psychosis" (2002, p. 1347), in that the perverse organisation does not break with reality but "confronts it in a false way" (2002, p. 1348). He postulates a close link between perversion and lies, with perversion found "on the opposite pole to truth" (2002, p. 1353).

Emphasis on object relations

The trend in reinterpreting the meaning of perversion is generally towards a relational understanding. As Parsons notes ". . . Psychoanalysis has moved from seeing [perversion] as defensive against instinctual derivatives to seeing it as defensive against object-relatedness" (Parsons, 2000, p. 40). He suggests that instead of the construction of sexuality based on drive as comprising source, aim, and object, there has been a shift in conception to source, aim, and quality of relatedness to the object. Khan also writes about perversion in terms of object relations (although with a sexual edge). He considers perversion to be a defence against relationship, giving the appearance of intimacy but lacking reciprocity, with the perverse person needing to control the relationship. He distinguishes those that "fuck from *desire*" from those that "fuck from *intent*" (Khan, 1979, p. 197).

In the relational interpretation of defence (Khan, 1979, p. 197; Parsons, 2000, p. 40) a range of anxieties can be incorporated (Mawson, 1999, p. 1; Steiner, 1993, pp. 10–11), including sexual anxieties (Freud, 1927e, p. 153).

As Ruth Stein states:

> perversion does not limit itself to the sexual perversions, but is rather a special case of perverse modes of object-relatedness and responses to the demands of reality which are perverse. Consequently, perversion often manifests itself as a disguised often sexualized, enactment of hatred and destructiveness which is actualized within a relational structure, what I call the "perverse pact". (Ruth Stein, 2005, p. 776)

This fits with Rosenfeld's (1971, p. 174) description of a highly organised destructive, narcissistic organisation within the psyche, comparable to the Mafia, that defensively works at retaining its power. Typical products of such systems would be negativism, including the negativistic caricature of object relations.

Phillips also accepts this broader view, emphasising the common characteristic of lack of empathy and misreading of the other in relationships and of reliance on perverse "prefigurings". He suggests that it is always perverse to think we know beforehand exactly what we desire, as this assumes the other "has nothing to offer us, that it brings nothing—or just rage and disappointment . . ." (Phillips, 1994, p. 65). He is describing encounters in which one person does not relate to the other as fully human.

Khan writes about "alienation" in object relations. He describes how, "The pervert puts an *impersonal object* between his desire and his accomplice: this *object* can be a stereotype fantasy, a gadget or a pornographic image. All three alienate the pervert from himself, as alas, from the object of his desire" (Khan, 1979, p. 9).

A modification of this view is Morgenthaler's (1988, p. 13) understanding of gradations of perversion on a continuum. He thinks of perversion as having a filling function, designed to assist a failing narcissistic development in early childhood, allowing the development of ego and libido to succeed. Perversion is seen as a "prosthetic completion" (1988, p. 14), bridging this inner contradiction between fantasy and reality which is due to lack of developmental integration. This intrasystemic organisation leads to gradations in quality of object relatedness from crystallisation of a perversion round an "inanimate, unformed, and undifferentiated object" to an "animate, well-defined, highly differentiated object" (1988, p. 16) which can offer a mature loving relationship. He sees most people as falling in the middle ground, having some dehumanising qualities in their relationships with others, but not experiencing the need to resort to sexual perversion.

Bach describes "one of the more ubiquitous perversions of everyday life" (Bach, 1991, p. 75) which the patient himself calls a "technical" relationship" (1991, p. 76), explaining that he really does not know "anything about people as human beings" (1991, p. 78). This is a sadomasochistic mode of relating that may not include *sexual* perversions but always includes either conscious or unconscious sadomasochistic fantasies. Bach regards such sadomasochistic relations as developmentally related to sexual perversions because they are a defence "against an attempt to repair some traumatic loss that has not been adequately mourned" (1991, p. 76).

Summary of theory so far

Cooper notes the "remarkable agreement among analysts on the psychodynamics of perversion" (Cooper, 1991, p. 23). This makes it possible to summarise the key areas of broad theoretical agreement concerning *sexual* perversion within psycho-analysis. The following is a summary of the theoretical positions included so far in this and the previous chapter, which should provide a basis for moving forwards towards an expanded understanding of perversion.

Sexual perversion is a deviation, of either aim or object, from adult genital sexuality (Freud, 1905d, p. 165). The existence of a *perverse psychic structure* is generally accepted, although this is variously conceived as a pact against reality (Ruth Stein, 2005, p. 793), a mental strategy (Kaplan, 1991, p. 9), an organised system of defences (Mawson, 1999, p. 1), or a psychic retreat (Steiner, 1993, pp. 10–11). The perverse structure acts as a *defence against Oedipal conflicts and anxieties*, particularly castration anxiety and guilt (Freud, 1919e; Gillespie, 1956, p. 398; Verhaeghe, 2004, pp. 127–128), also against recognition of the primal scene (McDougall, 1972, p. 378), and against confusion over sexual identity (Bak, 1968, p. 16; McDougall, 1972, p. 375; Rangell, 1991, p. 17). The defensive mechanisms employed are denial in the form of *disavowal* (Freud, 1927e, p. 153) of the maternal phallus, *splitting of the ego* (Gillespie, 1956, p. 402) so that only part progresses, *idealisation* of the pregenital self rather than the father (Chasseguet-Smirgel, 1974, p. 349), and *regression* to or *fixation* at a stage of infantile sexuality. Functioning of the perverse structure is characterised by *aggression and sadism* culminating in *triumph* (Kernberg, 1988, p. 1007; Mawson, 1999, pp. 1 & 7; Stoller, 1977, pp. 96–101), *addiction and compulsion* (Adler, 1986, p. 187; Kaplan, 1991, p. 10; Mawson, 1999, p. 6; McDougall, 1972, p. 372; Money, 1988; Steiner, 1993, p. 103–104), and *rigidity* (Coen, 1992, p. 224; Kaplan, 1991, p. 10; McDougall, 1972, p. 371; 1978, p. 198; Steiner, 1993, p. 27).

Moves within psycho-analysis towards expanding this theoretical model involve:

(a)   The inclusion of anxieties unrelated to sexual conflicts (Fairbairn, 1944, p. 89; Manninen & Absets, 2000, pp. 193–194).

(b)   Splitting the concept of perversion either horizontally into levels of severity (Meltzer, 1979, p. 134), or vertically into traits or areas of cognitive functioning (Arlow, 1991, pp. 63–65; Ermann, 2005, pp. 188–189; Money-Kyrle, 1968, pp. 692–693; Sánchez-Medina, 2002, pp. 1345–1353; Waddell & Williams, 1991, pp. 203–213) with consideration of the non-sexual meaning of a particular section.

(c)   Emphasising object relatedness (Bach, 1991, pp. 75–78; Khan, 1979, pp. 9 & 197; Morgenthaler, 1988, pp. 13–16; Parsons, 2000, p. 40; Phillips, 1994, p. 65; Ruth Stein, 2005, p. 776).

Further expansion of the traditional model

Despite some post-Freudian developments, there is still crystallisation and restriction of the concept of perversion and little acknowledgement of some important aspects of its meaning. The Freudian understanding of perversion is underpinned by Freud's theory of infantile sexuality, that in turn is supported by the paradigms of polymorphous perversity and the Oedipus complex. Both paradigms stir controversy. For example, Meltzer criticises Freud's theory as "more descriptive than metapsychological" (Meltzer, 1979, p. 66). Andrews and Brewin (2000, pp. 606–607), looking for evidence of Freud's theories generally, cite the work of Fisher and Greenberg (1996) that found only weak and indirect support for the notion of Oedipal conflicts, and no support for their impact on later development. Jung (1913, par. 293) questions whether polymorphous perversity exists at all, or was just Freud's theoretical assumption, since the theory is not based on observation of infants but is merely inferred from the analysis of adult patients.

In Freudian theory perversion is an inappropriate perseveration of pre-genital instinctual sexuality (developmental failure). In the traditional model, this developmental failure is combined with a delusional structure that disavows the reality of castration (intrapsychic deception). Both concepts, developmental failure and intrapsychic deception, can be strengthened by a broadening of their applicability, so they apply to relational quality more generally and not just to sexuality. To do this, I consider it essential to weaken the link between infantile sexuality and later non-sexual perversion. Although non-sexual perversion possesses many of the same unconscious dynamics as sexual perversion, it is *behaviourally* different and there seems no reason to assume that non-sexual perversion emanates from developmental problems in sexuality.

Within a more comprehensive theoretical framework, perversion could be seen as a response to early *relational* trauma. I will briefly summarise my conception of how perversion takes hold: in Chapter Seven this is fully elucidated, step by step. The process begins with the splitting off and intrapsychic projection of unbearable relational material (intrapsychic deception). Although this could result in processing and reintegration, in perversion reintegration fails, (developmental failure) and self-deception becomes established through the employment of a variety of defence mechanisms, particularly splitting, projection, and regression. The relational projection is then strengthened and further projected, templating external relationships and creating the dominance of one, consistently narrow, relational mode, that is vengefully imposed on others either sexually, bodily, or emotionally and cognitively. The specific mode of relating symbolises the intrapsychic projection, representing elements in microcosm of the original unbearable relational experience.

My formulation gives equal weight to all forms of perverse enactment, considering sexual perversion as the traditional, rather than the prime, example. Fogel takes the view that, "Freud used perversion as a paradigm to demonstrate the unique importance of infantile sexuality in psychic development" (Fogel, 1991, p. 1), but it is possible to reverse this idea and to consider sexuality as the paradigm that demonstrates the particular qualities of perversion, which might also be understood non-sexually. For example, Arlow's (1991, p. 63) assumption that deceptive traits are "parented" by sexual perversions, could be viewed as intrapsychic deception being causally implicated in both outcomes. Similarly, perverse thought, with a duality of truths, could be called either deception or self-deception. Its behavioural aspect is called "cognitive perversion" in Chapter Seven and presented as one type of non-sexual perversion. Perversion with a wider meaning will be subdivided in Chapter Seven, with examples of three types of manifestation of perverse psychic structure: (i) sexual, (ii) bodily, and (iii) emotional and cognitive perversion. (i) involves sexual action, (ii) involves action that is taken against the body but does not appear to be primarily sexual, and (iii) involves agency through thinking and feeling.

Many of the qualities described earlier in this chapter as characterising sexual perversion could also apply to an expanded model that includes non-sexual perversion. For example, Steiner's malignant narcissism, as part of a perverse psychic structure, could equally characterise non-sexual perversion. If early narcissistic damage is associated primarily with humiliation rather than sexuality, which in my view it is not difficult to envisage, Steiner's intrapsychic "perverse liaison" (Steiner, 1982, p. 250) is replicated vengefully in a varied range of external relationships. Giving implicit support to this wider interpretation, is Kernberg's (1990, pp. 325–326) conflation of pre-Oedipal and Oedipal conflicts in perversion, suggesting that sexuality is not the only source of conflict. Likewise the sexual/sadism link can be questioned. Some years ago the Home Office and the Prison Service commissioned a study to evaluate the Sex Offender Treatment Programme conducted in prisons in England and Wales since 1991. Sex offenders could be categorised in three groups: grievance-motivated offenders, sexually motivated offenders, and sadistically motivated offenders (Dillon-Hooper, 2007, p. 4). Although vengeful-ness might be present in all groups, sadism appears more restricted. Consistent with this study, although not evident within it, would be an unconscious reversal of power, with humiliation leading to venge-ful attack. A broader picture of vengefulness, including but not restricted to sexuality, is presented in Chapter Seven (Theoretical formulation—G).

My own reinterpretation also differs somewhat from the tradi-tional model in the functioning of defences. In Chapter Seven, I describe diphasic splitting as a response to trauma, with initial intrapsychic splitting and projection having a prospective value. Given sufficient resolution of conflict (Coen, 1992, p. 224), reintegra-tion of projected material is achieved. This projection is a "relational projection", meaning a projection of the self-in-relationship rather than a projection of part of the self. Failure to reintegrate through immaturity (pregenitality in the sexual sense) or lack of ego strength (including lack of imagination and fantasy), leads to the second stage in which the relational projection becomes a dominant part of the psyche which is rigidly projected externally, templating all relation-ships. This results in a narrow object range with lack of choice (Kaplan, 1991, p. 10), demand for compliance (McDougall's (1972, p. 378) symbolic castration), and associated compulsive behaviour (McDougall, 1972, p. 375).

Although writing as a sexologist and not about relationships more generally, Money (1988, pp. 127–137) neatly brings splitting and projection into a relational context that is particularly relevant to my reinterpretation. He suggests mapping idealised relationships with the concepts of normophilic and paraphilic lovemaps (he uses normophilia as an antonym of paraphilia). "A lovemap is defined as a personalized, developmental representation or template in the mind and in the brain that depicts the idealized lover and the idealized program of sexuoerotic activity with that lover as projected in imagery and ideation, or actually engaged in with that lover" (1988,

p. 127). He suggests rating lovemaps that are not normophilic as "hypophilic, meaning incomplete or insufficient; as hyperphilic, meaning too dominant or prevalent; or as paraphilic, meaning unlikely love, or love that is too peculiar and divergent from the given norm" (1988, p. 127). A lovemap is as personalised as a face or finger-print and is a repository of a person's sexuoerotic credenda and agenda. A credenda is "a memorandum of the complete inventory of imagery and ideation, separated or interconnected as in the story or drama of a dream or fantasy that may either induce or augment personal sexuoerotic arousal, heightening its intensity and facilitating the achievement of orgasm" (1988, p. 128). Credenda and agenda are sexuoerotically related in the same way as are a rehearsal and an actual dramatic performance, "one precedes and then becomes the other" (1988, p. 128). He believes that the paraphilic lovemap holds the key to the contents of a particular paraphilia (1988, p. 134) and suggests that each paraphilia has its own lovemap incorporating one of six stratagems for saving lust from extinction by cleaving it from love (1988, p. 136).

I adopt a similar idea to his credenda, that comes close to Parsons' (2000, p. 41) concept of position, meaning underlying psychic constel-lation (2000, p. 40). This acts in perversion as an internal template determining relational perception and behaviour and idealising a narrow relational mode. Money also links ideation with imagery which is key to my own formulation (Chapter Seven: Theoretical formulation—G).

If perversion is a way of treating others, an unempathic "tech-nique" of relating, it raises the issue of the other's consent. Camphausen (1991, p. 148) goes so far as to regard lack of consent as the only fixed attribute of perversion. The issue of consent led to homosexuality becoming declassified as a mental illness in the last edition of *DSM-II* (American Psychiatric Association, 1973). Although this was initially replaced with a category of ego-dystonic homosexu-ality, Kutchins and Kirk argue that consent should be an even greater determinant of pathology, and should cover heterosexuality that is "unwanted and a persistent source of distress" (Kutchins & Kirk, 1999, p. 15).

There is an acknowledgement that non-perverse relating requires containment of behaviour, whether it be sexuality (Goldberg, 2006, pp. 41–45), aggression (Kernberg, 1988, p. 1007), or just one's own desires and impulses as opposed to those of others (Camphausen, 1991, p. 148). This requirement demonstrates the need for a theoretical model that incorporates a clear turning point between potential perversion that is contained intrapsychically and actual perversion involving destructive behaviour towards others. There is a description in Chapter Seven (Theoretical model—D) of how the reintegration of intrapsychically projected relational material can prevent movement into perverse behaviour.

CHAPTER SIX

A Jungian perspective

Doubt truth to be a liar

Shakespeare, *Hamlet*, Act 2: Scene 2

C entral to Jungian theory is a holistic view of the psyche. This means the internal world is a vibrant system of interconnectedness, extending multi-dimensionally rather than through linear causal chains, into a living pattern of emergent self-organising structures. Jung uses the term *unus mundus* (unitary world) to describe the transcendent existence uniting the duality of mind (*psyche*) and matter (*physis*) (Jung, 1955, par. 660). Such a system is more than the assemblage of parts; it is continually growing and changing along with its elements (Senge, Scharmer, Jaworski, & Flowers, 2005, p. 5), and meaning is associated with this "experience of totality" (Jaffe, 1984, p. 13). Even if wholeness is unobtainable, it represents the goal and direction of individuation, with healthy development dependant on sacrifice or submission of the parts or elements for the purposes of the whole (L. Stein, 1966, p. 28). The following chapter describes how perversion, through its defensive and segmented nature, directly opposes this psychic integrity.

The physicist Capra (1982, pp. 396–397) compares the different conceptual approaches of Freud and Jung to that between classical and modern physics, between the mechanistic and the holistic paradigm. The Jungian, holistic paradigm is also characteristic of other theoretical systems. For example, the biochemist Sheldrake, who regards some of his own theories as complementary to those of Jung, postulates a "morphogenetic field" (Sheldrake, 1987, p. 76) of self-organising systems at all levels of complexity from cellular to whole organism. Each living system is a whole comprised of parts which are themselves whole at a lower level. He uses the term "morphic resonance" (1987, p. 98) to describe a dynamic evolutionary process, whereby every embodiment of a living system through its creation simultaneously contributes to a larger morphogenic field and to its evolution.

The specificity of perverse ideation and behaviour exemplifies this micro/macrocosmic equivalence (Chapter Seven).

Similarly, in the context of chaos theory, Briggs contrasts the logical, incremental, and predictable progression of a linear system with the acute sensitivity and constant change through internal and external fluctuation in a nonlinear system. ". . . they are so webbed with positive feedback that the slightest twitch anywhere may become amplified into an unexpected convulsion or transformation" (Briggs, 1992, p. 19). At the boundary of chaos and order, at any moment "the feedback in a dynamic system may amplify some unsuspected external or internal influence, displaying this holistic interconnection" (1992, p. 21). The system in microcosm is represented in fractals: "images of the way things fold and unfold, feeding back into each other and themselves" (1992, p. 23). Fractal scaling describes similar details on different scales with the system's whole movement taking place continuously at every level (1992, p. 23).

The holographic paradigm structures a similar world view. Zinkin describes how Jung uses modern physics as an analogy for psychic processes. In the paradigm of the hologram, "Any tiny fragment of the hologram will still reproduce the whole image" (Zinkin, 1987, p. 1). He cites the physicist Bohm, who asserts the primacy of wholeness: the whole organising the parts and the whole enfolded into the parts. A small part therefore contains the information of the whole (1987, p. 6). Interconnectedness thereby replaces a mechanistic order and causality does not depend on proximity in time and space. One implication that Zinkin highlights is the holistic working of the brain, with memory, even a discrete memory, spread throughout the brain rather than localised (1987, pp. 8–9). This microcosmic representation of the psyche within a dynamic unity is associated in Chapter Seven with initial positive moves towards psychic integration whose failure can result in perversion as an unconscious choice. Significantly, for the development of a Jungian understanding of perversion, the holographic paradigm and fractal scaling conform to the principle of symmetry, one of Matte Blanco's principles of unconscious logic. In the unconscious "all members of a set or class are treated as identical to one another *and to the whole set or class* and are therefore interchangeable . . ." (author's italics) (Matte Blanco, 1975, p. 39). It is a feature of reality poetically acknowledged by Blake:

To see a World in a Grain of Sand
And a Heaven in a Wild Flower,
Hold Infinity in the palm of your hand
And Eternity in an hour.

Blake, 2000, p. 135

A holistic approach presents the opportunity for behaviour associated with perversion to be viewed in more than one light: the perverse scenario might be seen not only as a distressing symptom but also as a creative composition. Indeed the artist Escher, renowned for his deceptive compositions, states that, "The artist's ideal is to produce a crystal-clear reflection of his own true self" (Escher, 2010, p. 4). "Compositions" are also one of the three categories into which the painter Kandinsky divided his works. Compositions were distinguished from "impressions" (observations of the natural world) and "improvisations" (spontaneous expressions of mood or feeling), in being inner visions with meticulous planning and intricate structure analogous to a symphony (Paul, 2006). This categorisation is helpful in understanding what perverse expression is and what it is not. Rigidity and exactness of repetition and lack of spontaneity immediately exclude it from the category of "improvisations"; it also lacks the freedom and feeling of an "impression"; whereas the inner vision, meticulous planning, and intricate structure of the "composition" are certainly present. But in actuality the perverse scenario is far from an imaginatively composed symphony, it is a largely unconscious conception and its fragmentary and dissociated nature denies full expression of the concerted orchestra of the psyche. Although perversion is not art, it is like art in being a subjective expression of a particular relationship to reality.

I would argue that a Jungian perspective can enhance our understanding of perversion and demonstrate how the concept is not adequately represented by the psycho-analytic model. Introducing this Jungian perspective involves adopting a broad understanding of the concept of libido, extending beyond the area of sexuality; linking of instinct through the collective unconscious to imagery and perceptive ideas; the acceptance of archetypal governance in psychic organisation and in defence mechanisms; and understanding of a futural sense in the psyche, including teleological directness in the creation of symptoms.

There are four significant areas of conceptual difference in Jungian, as compared with Freudian, theory that all have implications for an expansion of the theory of perversion. Each contributes to my theoretical formulation.

Conceptual differences

A Freudian template cannot easily be superimposed on Jungian theory for comparative purposes, nor vice versa, since different conceptions imply different perceptions. The principal differences between the two interpretive traditions can be divided into four areas of equivalence. The Jungian concept is the first in each of the following pairs:

(a) psychic energy and libido
(b) archetype and instinct
(c) collective and personal unconscious
(d) teleology and understanding of causation.

Each area of difference will be considered in turn with emphasis on how a Jungian interpretation might support a broader theory of perversion. In all four areas there are three levels at which a Jungian perspective might contribute:

(a) structurally—concerning the structure of the psyche
(b) functionally—relating to functioning within the psychic structure
(c) behaviourally—in terms of behavioural enactments.

First conceptual difference: psychic energy and libido

Jung criticises Freud's conception of sexuality as "uncommonly wide", since it includes not only "normal sexuality but all the perversions, and extends far into the sphere of psychosexual derivates. When Freud speaks of sexuality, it must not be understood merely as the sexual instinct" (Jung, 1908, par. 49). He accuses Freud of stretching sexual terminology, and contests his right to "designate as 'sexual'" (Jung, 1913, par. 262) early infantile phenomena such as sucking, which could be used later in life for sexual purposes without their origins being necessarily sexual.

Jung thinks of the basis of the personality as affectivity rather than sexuality. He might agree with McDougall that "There is little doubt that the leading 'erotogenic zone' is located in the mind!" (McDougall, 1991, p. 178). For him psychic energy is neutral, flowing between opposing poles, and resulting from opposites in tension (Jung, 1929a, par. 779). He also links psychic energy with the constitutional disposition of the individual and the intrapsychic structure of the unconscious. He broadens the psychoanalytic concept of libido, envisioning psychic energy as motivating a wider range of biological gratifications than Freud encompasses (Jung, 1913, par. 283), as well as showing concern for meaning through symbol formation, conceptualising, and cultural activity (Fordham, 1959, p. 20; Hauke, 2000, p. 52).

Jung agrees with Freud that "the beginnings of many tendencies which in later life are called 'perversions' ", are apparent in childhood (Jung, 1913, par. 258). Jung reluctantly accepts the term "perverse" to describe infantile sexual behaviour, recognising an "analogy with later perversions" which are connected to particular erogenous zones and show "anomalies which are so characteristic of children" (Jung, 1913, par. 245). As he finds no evidence for either a multiplicity of partial drives (polymorphous perverse disposition) or a diphasic sexual development as Freud describes (Frey-Rohn, 1974, p. 149), Jung prefers to think of infantile sexuality as "rudimentary and provisional" (Jung, 1913, par. 292). He maintains that the term "polymorphous perverse" is unjustifiably "borrowed from the psychology of neurosis and projected backwards into the psychology of the child" (1913, par. 293). He is accusing Freud of unnecessarily pathologising infancy (1913, par. 292) or of having a perverse understanding of infant development. Jung distinguishes striving for pleasure from sexual gratification, claiming that a child cannot be called perverse because he "does not yet know the normal sexual function" (1913, par. 259). He refers to the "alimentary libido" (1913, par. 290) needing to convert itself slowly into sexual libido during the course of child-hood, passing through two distinct stages, the phase of sucking, and the phase of displaced rhythmic activity. In the second stage, interest shifts from the oral zone to other orifices, and then to the skin, perhaps in particular regions of the body. The libido "continues its wanderings until it reaches the sexual zone" (1913, par. 291). Jung grounds the infantile libido in the body rather than in sexuality, making a distinc-tion between the two:

> The polymorphism of libidinal strivings at this period can be explained as the gradual migration of libido, stage by stage, away from the sphere of the nutritive function into that of the sexual func-tion. Thus the term "perverse" . . . can be dropped . . . . (Jung, 1913, par. 292)

He replaces "polymorphous perverse" with the more neutral "poly-valent germinal disposition", a term which is not listed in the *General Index of Jung's Collected Works* (Read, Fordham, Adler, & McGuire, 1979) and hides almost unnoticed in the foreword to the 1915 second edition of *Psychic Conflicts in a Child* (Jung, 1915). He argues that:

> The fact that adult sexuality grows out of this polyvalent germinal disposition does not prove that infantile sexuality is "sexuality" pure and simple. I therefore dispute the rightness of Freud's idea of the "polymorphous-perverse" disposition of the child. It is simply a *poly-valent* disposition. (Jung, 1915, p. 5)

In the 1938 foreword to the third edition of the same study (Jung, 1938, p. 7) Jung elaborates the point:

> To document the polyvalent germinal disposition of the child with a sexual terminology borrowed from the stage of fully-fledged sexuality is a dubious undertaking. It means drawing everything else in the child's make-up into the orbit of sexual interpretation; so that on the one hand the concept of sexuality is blown up to fantastic proportions and becomes nebulous, while on the other hand spiritual factors are seen as warped and stunted instincts. Views of this kind lead to a ratio-

nalism which is not even remotely capable of doing justice to the essential polyvalence of the infantile disposition. Even though a child may be preoccupied with matters which, for adults, have an undoubtedly sexual complexion, this does not prove that the nature of the child's preoccupation is to be regarded as equally sexual. (Jung, 1938, p. 7)

"Polyvalent germinal disposition" can usefully replace "polymorphous perversity" for a broader understanding of the beginnings of all psychic development, not only of sexual functions, providing a key to the expansion of the psycho-analytic theory of perversion through Jungian concepts to include non-sexual perversion. The origin of perversion, in this broader sense, does not necessarily lie within the narrow confines of infantile *sexual* development but may relate to a much broader range of early *relational* development, at a time of infantile bodily dependence, when relational trauma becomes embodied and is incorporated as a body memory.

Such a re-conceptualisation allows for consideration of sexual and non-sexual perversion as ontogenetically allied and capable of being incorporated in the same theoretical structure. The body is the site of overlap between Freudian and Jungian theory and arguably also between sexual and non-sexual perversion. "Bodily perversion", involving bodily dominance and imposition without obvious sexual intent, is the grey area between sexual perversion and cognitive and emotional perversion where there is no essential sexual or bodily involvement.

Second conceptual difference: archetype and instinct

For Jung the instincts transform along a continuum between the collective unconscious and consciousness. They move away from "the hallmarks of instinct: automatism, non-susceptibility to influence, all-or-none reaction", associated with "a more primitive (archaic-mythological) level", and enter into the adaptive process going forward in consciousness, through which "they personalize and rationalize themselves to the point where a dialectical discussion becomes possible" (Jung, 1947/1954, par. 384). Jung compares this range to the sequence of colours in the spectrum. Fordham pursues this analogy, identifying the imperceptible ultra-violet and infra-red areas of the spectrum as unconscious instinct and spirit (Fordham, 1988, p. 219).

In Jungian theory archetypes belong within the deepest level of the unconscious, the collective unconscious. They are universal, inherited, and non-representable prefigurative dispositions, the timeless constants of human nature and the product of millions of years of evolution (Jung, 1919, par. 270). As species-specific patterning structures, they give rise to shared archetypal perceptual predispositions (1919, par. 274) through which we form symbolic fantasies governing our perception of the world (Stevens, 2002, p. 82). Knox describes archetypes as "nuclei of unconscious meaning ... the unconscious is not merely an accumulation of all that is unacceptable to the conscious mind but plays an active role as a co-contributor to the construction of symbolic meaning in the human psyche" (Knox, 2004, p. 59). This accords with Gordon's interpretation of archetypes as "psychological possibilities" (Gordon, 1993, p. 20) bearing a striking resemblance to Klein's unconscious phantasies (mental expression of the instinct), a connection also made by Astor (1995, p. 20).

Through inheritance, both archetype and instinct link the individual to the species and the present to the past, but conceptually they are antonyms reflecting conflicting perspectives. Instinct belongs in the scientific, material world; archetypes belong in the unconscious. This difference highlights the divergent perspectives of Freud and Jung. As Steele states, "Freud defined human consciousness against the background of natural biological processes, Jung against historical symbolic processes" (Steele, 1982, p. 233). This difference in perspective is between heritage and inheritance, between culture and biology. Initially Freud also explores "archaic regression" in a letter written to Jung in 1910 (Freud, 1974a, p. 291), and "phylogenetic memory" in another letter to Jung of 1911 (Freud, 1974b, p. 449), but he later moves away from Jung's ideas, regarding these phenomena as "memory traces" (Freud, 1950a[1896], p. 233), and deciding that instinct is "the concept on the frontier-line between the somatic and the mental" (Freud, 1911a, p. 74). Archetypes form a psychosomatic model in a different way from Freud's conception of instinct. They are bi-polar and bi-valent, with a biological/instinctual pole and a spiritual/imaginal pole (Mahlberg, 1987; Stevens, 2002, p. 52; Von Franz, 1974, p. 4). Jung regards archetypes as the "meaning" of instinct.

The operation of three specific archetypes is significant in my formulation of perversion.

The self, is the organiser of the psyche, which is ". . . not only the centre but also the whole circumference which embraces both conscious and unconscious" (Jung, 1936b, par. 44). In perversion the integrity of the self is compromised, as a split off relational projection assumes dominance, destabilising the psyche and perverting psychic development. Extreme defences are deployed to protect the self at the expense of psychic growth and wholeness. *The shadow,* as the darker reflection of the psyche, "the thing a person has no wish to be" (Jung, 1946, par. 470), exercises a gravitational pull. Getting to know the shadow is a healthy alternative to rejecting or being overwhelmed by it and adopting a shadow identity. As Hillman, states, "To be raped into the underworld is not the only mode of experiencing it" (Hillman, 1979, p. 49). Robert Stein (1973, pp. 55–63) stresses the need for the child to integrate, learn, and understand the shadow, and Cowan also believes that embracing the shadow is not necessarily destructive. She describes instead, "a dance-embrace, with timing and rhythm, give-and-take. Experiencing the shadow means accepting it lives within us—letting it, and thus ourselves, live" (Cowan, 1982, pp. 37–38). She conceives of the shadow as a psychopomp or guide to the nether regions, leading us back to our origins, to the archetypes at the centre of our complexes and foundation of our personalities (1982, p. 38). *The trickster,* ". . . a collective shadow figure, a summation of all the inferior traits of character in individuals" (Jung, 1954, par. 484), is evident in the paradoxes, deceits, ironies, and subterfuge implicit in both sexual and non-sexual perverse enactments.

Image

In his autobiography Jung writes, "The years when I was pursuing my inner images were the most important in my life—in them everything essential was decided" (Jung, 1967, p. 225). This gives a clear indication of the importance of imagery in Jungian theory which ensures that "thinking" ideas do not exclude "perceptive" ideas. In his typology Jung regards sensation and intuition as the perceptive, information gathering modes of the psyche. Holmes (2010, p. 583), researching in the area of experimental psychopathology, argues that to understand more about the basic processes of underlying psychological disorders we need to know much more about how we think in images, rather than just in words. She points to the strong link between mental imagery and emotion and the little that is known about imagery as a mechanism in emotional disorders. For example, imagery can manifest itself in devastating flashbacks and flash-forwards.

Archetypal images for Jung are not visual representations of drives, or preconceptions of general ideas as conceived by Money-Kyrle (1971, p. 105), but part of a networking access to the collective unconscious. Imagination involves the clustering of images produced in association with other mental processes such as past experiences, memories, thoughts, intentions, and emotions. Gordon defines such an image as "a mental representation of a sensuous experience in the absence of an actual stimulus" (Gordon [1983–1984], p. 10). She observes that Winnicott (1945, p. 141) comes very close to the idea of archetypes when he suggests that images exist prior to and before an actual experience, such as the infant encountering the maternal breast.

Archetypes are known by their imagery, by emotion, or through phantasy, and have a numinosity that Frey-Rohn attributes to their representation of "typical situations in life" (Frey-Rohn, 1974, p. 95). She is presenting the archetypal image as a governor of personal imagery, that opens imagery up to dual interpretation, both theoretically and clinically. Astor (1995, p. 27) distinguishes this difference clinically, associating the personal interpretation with reductive analysis, and the impersonal with the symbolic. But since the personal and archetypal are so inseparably bound, Hillman questions the term "archetypal" in relation to inner images since all such images have the archetypal qualities of "dramatic structure, symbolic universality, strong emotion . . ." (Hillman, 1991a, p. 26), making the adjective redundant.

Jung identifies Oedipal drama (integral to the psycho-analytic theory of sexual perversion) with imagery, describing it as taking in "the individual's own psyche", where the "parents" are not parents at all but only their images; they are representations which have arisen from the conjunction of parental peculiarities with the individual disposition of the child" (Jung, 1911, par. 505). Jung experiences this personally when in 1909 Freud dismisses him as his analyst, perhaps fearing loss of his own authority. This inspires in Jung an image of his killing the primal father. Hogenson regards this as vindicating the Oedipus complex "through image and projection [Jungian] rather than word and repression [Freudian]" (Hogenson, 1994, p. 147), since for both Freud and Jung, there is a projection of a primal image constituted in the unconscious, and projection rather than repression is the constituting mechanism of the psyche.

Jung finds support for his belief in the importance of imagery in the emerging science of ethology. His understanding of archetypes as internal organisers as well as systems of readiness for action (Jung, 1927, par. 53) is supported by the work of ethologists Tinbergen and Lorenz (Burkhardt, 2005), and more recently in discoveries by evolutionary psychologists and psychiatrists of neuropsychic propensities virtually indistinguishable from archetypes (Stevens, 2003, p. 255). Innate release mechanisms (IRMs) are perceptual stimuli, or images, triggering action and could be regarded as the extraverted behavioural end of the archetype in any particular species (Stevens, 2006, p. 83). Gordon ([1983–1984], p. 24) links the two central ethological concepts of innate fixed pattern and innate release mechanism, concluding that there must exist a potential *archetypal* image which then programmes the organism to respond in a certain manner when it encounters an object that matches this potential image ([1983–1984], pp. 9–10).

Jung considers this process to be more metaphorical in human beings, with fantasy images presenting as symbolic expressions of archaic structures in the psyche, even when they appear to represent only the personal (Jung, 1916b, par. 462). He becomes increasingly aware that the meaning of primitive sexual expression is in the unknown symbolic content of the image. Stevens goes further in believing that it would be more accurate to reconceptualise sexuality as "an archetypal system [rather] than as mere 'drive' or 'instinct' in view of its universality, its numinosity, and its power" (Stevens, 2002, p. 229). This understanding can be applied to sexual perversion, in which destructive relational behaviour becomes addictive, being shaped and triggered by a combination of imagery and associated affect. Although a human being might appear to have greater choice than an animal reacting to an IRM, the compulsion to respond to an external stimulus corresponding to an internal image can be overwhelming. Spinoza recognises this power when he states, "As long as a man is affected by the image of anything, he will contemplate the thing as present, although it does not exist". (Spinoza, 2001, pp. 112–113).

In perversion the present is linked to the past as the archetypal links to the personal, and imagery combines with affect in defining a specific mode of relating. There is no indication in ethology that the imagery involved in the shaping and triggering process applies only to sexuality. Similarly, in the human sphere, there is no theoretical assumption that archetypal governance of the personal unconscious applies only to instinct. If *non-sexual* material in the personal unconscious is subject to archetypal governance, where there is a weak or fragmented ego, this material will also be vulnerable to overdetermination by archetypal processes: this is a feature of non-sexual perversion.

Third conceptual difference: collective unconscious and personal unconscious

This is perhaps the most significant conceptual difference in terms of a theoretical understanding of perversion. Jungian theory emphasises the connection between the individual and the collective, and similarly between the personal and the deeper collective unconscious. Whereas the Freudian unconscious is a place of repression, of "immoral-egoistic, sadistic, perverse or incestuous—wish-impulses" (Freud, 1943, p. 73), Jung sees it as a necessary foundation for positive development, which also contains the "contents of the collective unconscious [that] have never been in consciousness, and therefore have never been individually acquired" (Jung, 1936a, par. 88). As Kalsched states, it is a "one-sided extraverted idea" (Kalsched, 1999, p. 466) that inner objects derive only from the internalisation of outer objects.

Symbolisation and the transcendent function

For Jung, symbolisation is perhaps the highest order of human processes. "A symbol does not define or explain, it points beyond itself to a meaning that is darkly divined yet still beyond our grasp" (Jung, 1926, par. 644). He distinguishes a symbol from a sign in its representation of the unknown (Astor, 1995, p. 29; Hauke, 2000, p. 193). Giegerich describes a symbol as the "unfinished embryonic form of a meaning" (Giegerich, 2004, p. 11), a sense of "in-ness" (2004, p. 12). The symbol dies when its meaning is clarified and it is comprehended conceptually. Gordon believes Jung makes an implicit assumption that "every phenomenon can be a symbol in as far as it entails otherness and something additional which is somehow fore-known or foreshown or of which one has an inkling" (Gordon, 1993, p. 69). This contrasts with the Freudian understanding of symbols as products of repression directly reducible to already experienced events or wishes of a predominantly sexual nature. These are "substi-tuted formulations" (Stevens, 1998, p. 8), designed to disguise the meaning of the ideas they represent, in the way dream symbolism becomes the guardian of sleep (Freud, 1900a, p. 411).

Symbolisation is the mediating process of the transcendent func-tion, that facilitates a transition from one psychological attitude or condition to another. "The transcendent function represents a linkage between real and imaginary, or rational and irrational data" (Samuels, Shorter, & Plaut, 1986, p. 150), bridging the gulf between conscious-ness and the unconscious. It is the ability to galvanise the positive and creative possibilities of opposites by transcending their oppositional status. This connectivity is a key process in the development or avoid-ance of perverse psychopathology. The transcendent function oper-ates through the mutually compensatory relationship of creative formulation and conscious understanding. "Out of this union emerge new situations and new conscious attitudes" (Williams, 1983, pp. 65–66). Hillman regards every psychic event as an identity of at least two positions and thus "symbolic, metaphorical and never one-sided" (Hillman, 1979, p. 80; see also Gordon, 1993, p. 191; Jung, 1939, par. 524). Such transcendence does not have the either/or antagonism of the traditional Freudian conscious–unconscious relationship (Hauke, 2000, p. 52), but is an active contributor to the meaning-making process through consummation of the union of conscious and unconscious contents.

Stevens (1998) identifies the psychic processes involved in symbol formation as resemblance (analogy, with simile and metaphor), condensation (many meanings in one configuration), and the micro-cosmic principle, also described by Briggs (1992), in which the macro-cosm is represented in the microcosm. Stevens (1998, p. ix) takes both a psychobiological and evolutionary perspective, seeing symbols as produced through interaction between phylogenetically prepared propensities and personal experiences. He describes symbols as both "intuitive concepts" and "living entities" (1998, p. 41) and he points to the adaptive role of archetypal symbols in guiding the development of our species (1998, p. 11).

The transformative power of symbolic representation is integral to a Jungian perspective on perversion, with the transcendent function making connections that create meaning. This process is critical to the unconscious decision to face the terrors that threaten the self, rather than opt for a defensive route towards perversion. Both Cowan and Robert Stein emphasise the need for psychic balance; since any part of the psyche that is dissociated may eventually assume destructive power over the psychic system as a whole. Perversion can be regarded as perversion of the transcendent function, since it endorses separation, dissociation, and lack of connectedness. This results in loss of identity, not just sexual identity as described by Manninen and Absets (2000, p. 193), McDougall (1972, p. 375), and Rangell (1991, p. 17) in relation to sexual perversion, but total self-identity which is dependent on the integrity of the psyche.

Myth, metaphor, and narrative

The human propensity to symbolise indicates the importance of myth, metaphor, and narrative in Jungian psychology, which differs from the Freudian scientific world-view in which no knowledge is derived from revelation, intuition, or divination (Freud, 1933a, p. 159). For Freud mysticism is a "closed book" (Freud, 1961, p. 389) with his own psychology of the unconscious providing an explanation of the origins of mythology; although he does adopt the myths of Oedipus and Narcissus for theoretical use.

Metaphorical language is arguably a particularly effective way of linking body, affect, and image, and therefore of understanding the roles of mind and body in perverse enactments. "Analytical psychology works to a great extent by analogy because only through analogy did Jung feel he could reliably reproduce the sense of the systems he was trying to understand" (Steele, 1982, p. 325). With oppositional but complementary inner and outer realities in tension, life is "crazy and meaningful at once" Jung (1934, par. 65). The mythological cosmos with its knowledge, laws, customs, order, and structure, contrasts with the chaos from which it differentiated, a development comparable to consciousness becoming differentiated from the unconsciousness (Jacoby, 1993, pp. 5–7).

Midgley (2003, pp. 1, 24, & 31) understands myths as "imaginative patterns" and "networks of powerful symbols" (2003, p. 1) that are central to life and to science, since they shape meaning and significance, uniting the objective and subjective, the internal and the external, providing a context for rationality. The linguist, Kövecses (2000, p. 17), goes so far as to claim that it is impossible to conceptualise most aspects of the emotions in other than metaphorical terms. Hillman adopts the same stance towards psychopathology, believing that, "Only in mythology does pathology receive an adequate mirror, since myths speak with the same distorted, fantastic language" (Hillman, 1991b, p. 146).

Hogenson considers myth as probably the most important way in which people comprehend the world. He affirms Jung's theory of the myth as a symbol and a guide for the psyche in its search for meaning, projecting into the future as well as pointing back to the past. He not only considers this understanding to be concordant with the mind's cognitive structures, but sees demythologising, rather than mythologising, as an invitation to neurosis or psychosis (Hogenson, 1994, pp. xiv & 89). This is possibly the opposite of the traditional Freudian position in which myth making can be viewed as regressive. Hogenson's view echoes Jung's belief that certain contents are constellated in the unconscious but cannot be assimilated through lack of apperceptive concepts to frame them. Experience of fairy-tales, legends, and religious concepts helps to develop this integrative facility (Jung, 1951b, par. 259), establishing deep patterns of understanding. Mogenson considers that "Man's capacity to change his skin, shift his metaphors, and wear a variety of garments protects him in a fashion that allows him to sample more of the stimuli emanating from the external world than any other creature" (Mogenson, 2005, pp. 119–120).

The fine balance between healthy and damaging uses of the imagination appears in relation to perversion in the following chapter. It could be said that behind every case of perverse psychopathology is a narrative which, like a myth, symbolises the state of the psyche both in the understanding of experience and in the need for expression. This means that every perverse act is embedded in a narrative and has its own myth. In the medical field this perspective on pathology is adopted by Charon (1993, p. 147–159) who coins the term "narrative medicine", in contrast to evidence-based medicine. As a teacher, she encourages doctors to "read" and understand their patients' stories through literary studies, believing that narrative enables communication by imbuing thoughts and sensations with meaning.

Hillman regards a fundamental tenet of archetypal psychology to be the interchangeability of mythology and psychology. He calls mythology "a psychology of antiquity" and psychology a "mythology of modernity" (Hillman, 1979, p. 23). By implication, psychology and mythology have the same ingredients but develop to accommodate different modes of understanding and forms of meaning. He suggests that archetypes themselves might be thought of as metaphors (Hillman, 1991a, p. 23), in keeping with his appreciation of psychology as a "poetic basis of mind" (T. Moore, 1991, p. 15) and with Jung's own re-visioning of psychology. Hillman's approach is not to match the themes in mythology and art to similar themes in life but to see every fragment of life and every dream as myth and poetry. As Moore's editorial comment confirms, for Hillman "psychoanalytic concepts and ideas have to be heard as expressions of imagination and read as metaphors" (T. Moore, 1991, p. 16).

In perversion the myth making capacity is severely curtailed through the disabling of the transcendent function and the lack of intrapsychic connectivity. This leaves the psyche dominated by an impoverished and simplistic fantasy based on early trauma, a deceptive narrative through which all relational encounters are translated. Oscar Wilde once stated, through his character Lady Stutfield, that "The secret of life is to appreciate the pleasure of being terribly, terribly deceived" (Wilde, [1893]1996, p. 62). For someone who is driven to revenge by their own unconscious hatred of having being deceived, and who is in the grip of a perverse psychic structure, the opposite is true. The pleasure comes from the terrible, terrible deception of others. This easily combines with flagrant self-deception that eludes self-examination and self-understanding.

Defences

Jung places less emphasis on pathology than Freud, and gives defences a more positive role in the adaptive functioning of the psyche. Theorising about the dangers we might need to avoid and utilising appropriate defences is a healthy part of forming a picture of ourselves in relation to the world. Schulz describes such theorising as an "evolutionary utility" (Schulz, 2010, p. 97) which involves "making models of the world" (2010, p. 99) and is essential to staying alive. All of the defences described in the following chapter as integral to perversion, have potentially positive value for the psyche, but are capable of being perverted for damaging, or ultimately destructive, purposes.

The principal defences of the perverse psychic structure are splitting, projection, dissociation, denial, idealisation, regression, and repetition compulsion. The functioning of projection and regression are demonstrated in action, from a Jungian perspective, in the following chapter. The others defences are essentially entwined.

Projection, rather than Freudian repression, is the primary Jungian defence (Hogenson, 1994, pp. 118–127), that Williams links from a Jungian viewpoint with the indivisible relationship between the personal and collective unconscious. She claims that "nothing in the personal experience needs to be repressed unless the ego feels threatened by its archetypal power and that the archetypal activity which forms the individual's myth is dependent on material supplied by the personal unconscious" (Williams, 1973, p. 79). In perversion, projection is a particularly powerful and consistent defence since all external relationships are subjected to stereotyped templating, and experienced only through a specific narrow range of projected relational material.

Jung presumes two levels of defences and two levels of severity of dissociation. At the less severe, or neurotic level, functional unity is undisturbed, but at the deeper defensive level there is a destruction of architecture and dissociation is unsystematic (Jung, 1958, par. 557). Kalsched believes that Freud fails to consider such primitive defences, ignoring the type of defensive reaction when the essential core of the person is threatened with extinction by unbearable affect; when "affects are dissociated, encapsulated, evacuated into the body (later to appear as physical symptoms) or acted out in a blind 'repetition compulsion' " (Kalsched, 1998, p. 84). In such cases there is a breakdown of coherent inner world structures and organising affect-images (archetypes). Following Leopold Stein (1966), Kalsched calls defences at this deeper level defences of the self (Kalsched, 1998, p. 85). Their pervasiveness contrasts with the psycho-analytic model of defences of the self described by Alexander and Friedman as "emergency measures of caring for the self" (Alexander & Friedman, 1980, p. 368), although Affeld-Niemeyer (1995, p. 26) does attribute these defences with similar qualities to the deeper Jungian defences; extreme defensiveness with an inability to think, a numbing of feelings and affects, and a suspension of the symbolising process.

The operation of extreme defences in response to early trauma is integral to perversion. Kalsched (1998) compares the archetypal anxiety of early trauma to a lightning bolt hitting the body. One part of the ego regresses to the infantile period, and another part progresses, precociously adapting to the outer world Kalsched (1996, pp. 2–5). These two parts comprise a self-care system, "the progressed part caretaking the regressed part" (1996, p. 3) by isolating it from reality and attacking links between body and mind. The self-care system will resort to defences including dissociation and addiction to achieve this end, attacking the symbolic function (Jung, 1958, par. 559). This may leave the person unable to play or symbolise, stuck in a repetition-compulsion of self-defeating behaviour. Kalsched describes how the defences associated with trauma are personified as archetypal daimonic images representing the psyche's self-portrait of its defensive operations. Fragments of consciousness arrange themselves according to archetypal patterns, particularly dyads and syzygies (pairs of opposites) made up of personified beings. Importantly, Kalsched (1996, p. 16) regards resistance to re-experiencing feelings of dependency as the perverse goal of the self-care system. In making this connection, he is implicitly categorising the use of such severe dissociative defences, all of which characterise perversion, as an attachment disorder. He shows the link between defence and detachment that is central to perverted relationships, where increase in perceived threat means defensiveness is ratcheted up, with archetypal defences creating a deeper dissociation.

Wilkinson (2005, p. 484), writing at the interface of analytical psychology and neurology, cites Chefetz's (2000) research findings, that analytic patients who use dissociation as a defence tend to have more non-verbal material. She also cites Schore (2005) and Devinsky (2000), from whose work she concludes that if trauma occurs before the age of three, the processing capacity of the left hemisphere that enables explicit recall, is not yet available, so the processing of early traumatic memory is largely limited to imagery, which is associated with the right brain (Wilkinson, 2005, p. 487). These research findings point to the importance of imagery, as opposed to language, in defensive functions. This differs from the Freudian understanding of the use of imagery, such as in dreams, where it serves to *overcome* censorship (Hogensen, 1994, p. 106).

The next chapter will show how very painful personal experience can lead to a skewed interpretation of the whole world of relationships. There is a point in the establishment of perverse psychic functioning beyond which psychic defences no longer allow a narrow and biased interpretation of the world to be revisited for review and reconsideration. Uncertainty is treated as if it were dangerous rather than essentially human, so a subjective truth is established. There is no sense that this truth is wrong since, as Schulz (2010, p. 18) observes, there is no experience of being wrong, being wrong feels like being right. This unconscious sense of rightness is not counterbalanced by a conscious appreciation of alternative perspectives as held by other people, so the power of unconscious conviction is unrestrained in fuelling vengeful action. There is then no possibility to learn from mistaken understandings, the perverse psychic disposition lacks this flexibility.

Complexes

Complexes are affectively toned clusters of associated ideas, characteristic of normal development. The complex has a nucleus with two components, the dispositional and the environmental; reaction to current experiences being determined by past experience and also by innate disposition. Complexes may be conscious, unconscious, or in the collective unconscious (Fordham, 1959, p. 23), but always enclose an archetypal nucleus that carries archaic meaning and constitutional pattern.

The complex is so significant to Jung that in the 1930s he renames analytical psychology "complex psychology", meaning the psychology of complexities or complex psychical systems (Shamdasani, 2003, p. 13). There is no equivalent in psycho-analysis to these layered complexes (Frey-Rohn, 1974, pp. 25 & 35), which Hillman describes as "the twists and turns in our nature" (Hillman, 1979, p. 129).

Knox understands complexes as analogous to Bowlby's internal working models (Bowlby, [1969](1999)) in attachment theory, which can become "implicit, unconscious maps of our accumulated experience of past relationships with key attachment figures that we draw on to anticipate and understand new human encounters and relationships" (Knox, 2004, p. 67). She points to the relevance of Schacter's (1996) concept of implicit memory whereby "past experiences unconsciously influence our perception, thoughts and action" (Knox, 2004, p. 65) through the formation of abstract generalised memory patterns, rather than specific records of particular events. She cites as relevant analogies Bartlett's (1932) concept of schemas organising past reactions and experiences; Johnson-Laird's (1989) development of Craik's (1943) internal models as determinants of perception and experience, which he regards as internal symbols providing a mental map; and Fonagy's (2001) work on the acquisition of meaning through the use of mental models rather than formal logic (Knox, 2004, pp. 64–65). Although less firmly bedded in theory, Money (1988, pp. 127–137, Chapter 3.5) and Parsons (2000, pp. 40–41, Chapter 3.3.2) both describe a similar process. Saunders and Skar (2001, pp. 311–312), who define an archetype as a class of complexes falling within the same category, suggest that complexes are formed by mind self-organisation. This supports Jung's understanding that splitting and complex formation are a healthy part of the psyche, and often not pathological (Jung, 1937, par. 253), although in perversion, it is through these complexes that the templating of relationships is patterned.

The ego is one such complex but it can also appropriate and use other complexes. Of relevance to perversion, Knox (2004, p. 57) describes how complexes without the ego and its self-reflection, function automatically with a compulsive quality. She considers that the network or matrix of complexes, sometimes working defensively, with no identifiable boundaries between thoughts and feelings, fits contemporary understanding in neuroscience better than theories of drives, death instinct, or unconscious fantasy (2004, p. 67). She finds support for considering the psyche as structurally and functionally compartmentalised, with "fragmentary personalities" or "splinter psyches", within which there is perception, feeling, volition, and intention. This likens complexes to Searles' multiple identity processes, although Searles conceives of a personalistic source rather than Jung's archetypal origin (Sedgwick, 1993, p. 13).

With a similar conception, Redfearn considers subpersonalities to be the Jungian equivalent of internal objects or part objects, but contrasting with them in that subpersonalities are based on innate patterns of perception and behaviour (Redfearn, 1994, pp. 295–300). With most human activity consisting of interaction between bits of people (subpersonalities), as part of normal as well as pathological functioning (1994, pp. 296 & 305), he conceives of the ego and the id behaving "as two distinct persons" (1994, p. 285) with wills of their own. He also considers bodily states to be the locus of excitation, such as "the devouring part of the self" establishing itself as a subpersonality (1994, p. 294). He refers to the migratory nature of the I, and uses the term "ego-flitting" (moving house in Yorkshire dialect) to describe how the ego becomes possessed by different subpersonalities (1994, p. 307). Although this offers theoretical support in relation to the dissociative nature of perversion, my own understanding of the split off psychic content in perversion is that it is essentially *relational* and therefore neither a splinter psyche nor a subpersonality. It could, however, be regarded as a specific type of relational complex, or a composite of material from two or more complexes. With no existing name for this concept, in the following chapter I introduce two new terms to cover different stages of its functioning.

Psyche/soma

The Jungian model of the mind presumes a psychosomatic unity (Astor, 1995, p. 41) with the "psychoid" as the basic substance which, "in the course of personal and collective development, differentiates into matter or spirit or body and soul" (Gordon, 1993, p. 16). Psyche and soma are, therefore, united through archetypal symbolism (Meier, 1986, pp. 179, 183–184, & 240).

Psychosomatic disorders are bodily representations of the relationship between consciousness and the unconscious, which in Jungian terms includes the collective unconscious. This idea of conscious/unconscious relationship differs somewhat from the view of Green from the Paris School of Psychosomatics who describes how "... the psychosomatic patient puts his soma and external reality in communication, while crushing everything that pertains to the mind" (Green, 2010, p. 5).

Kradin relates a deficit in early nurturing with psychosomatic symptoms, conceptualising such symptoms as encapsulated psychoses, invasions of "the objective psyche into waking consciousness" (Kradin, 1997, p. 407), alongside normal ego functions, and Robert Stein (1976, p. 67) regards somatic symptoms to be as much a manifestation of a psychic reality as of a bodily reality, equating them clinically to dream imagery. The philosopher Johnson uses the term "body" to mean "the embodied origins of imaginative structures of

understanding, such as image schemata and their metaphorical elab-
orations" (Johnson, 1992, p. xv), believing in the indispensability of
embodied human understanding for meaning and rationality. This
idea is particularly important for perversion since it provides a link
between the internal (body and mind) and external action through use
of the body. Sexual perversion is manifestly a psychosomatic disorder
involving both psychic disturbance and bodily expression. It is
arguable that some non-sexual perversions also develop through early
negative body experiences of psychic or physical pain, or deprivation,
and could also be classified as psychosomatic in this sense.

In its bodily representation of unbearable relationship, perversion
bears a resemblance to hysteria, another bodily expression of such
interest diagnostically that it leads Breuer and Freud to early developments of the psycho-analytic method (Hauke, 2000, p. 177). Hauke
highlights the power of hysterical symptoms for these early, often
powerless, patients, showing how the experience of power is medi-
ated through their somatic symptoms (2000, p. 179). He describes
Jung's theory of emotional conflict, with splitting and investment in
fantasy resulting from powerlessness to act effectively in the outside
world (2000, p. 185), and suggests that hysterical symptoms "may be
viewed as an attempt to create 'I', a meaningful self derived from the
feeling of power . . . staged as a drama involving the whole body. In
this sense the symptoms seem to compensate for a weak or missing
sense of 'I' or ego . . ." (Hauke, 2000, p. 189). Although this is a
description of hysteria, the same compensatory assumption of power
through bodily action and retreat into fantasy is present in sexual
perversion. It is also arguable that the same dynamic of rebellion
against domination or deprivation, experienced as powerlessness and
theft of freedom for psychic development, motivates non-sexual
perversion. The power of deceptiveness might also be understood in
terms of tricksterish compensatory behaviour for feelings of powerlessness (Jung, 1954, par. 458).

Sidoli demonstrates a detailed clinical and theoretical understanding of how severe psychosomatic and dissociative defensive structures, such as those characterising perversion, develop in infancy. She
relates somatisation to the shadow, distinguishing the collective
shadow, that "pertains to the psychosomatic realm and is shaped by
one's earliest infantile affective experiences" (Sidoli, 2000, p. 71), from
the personal shadow, that emerges during the Oedipal phase. She

refers to splitting as the most common early defence mechanism, separating good and bad feeling, with the bad projected onto the mother/environment and the good kept inside. When there is regression, the ego weakens and "can fall back into being possessed by the shadow archetype's primitive contents" (2000, p. 73). She also describes shadow contents taking possession of the body, and becoming somatised in destructive illnesses or in perversions, when the ego disintegrates and the ego complex is gripped by the shadow (2000, pp. 73–74). She places the roots of the collective shadow in instinctual drives and affective responses located in the body and usually discharged in activity. If the infant has a mother/care-giver functioning as an auxiliary ego-consciousness when he is in states of overwhelming affective pressure, she modifies, contains, and transforms such affects into manageable emotional states so that eventually the child can think about them and then subsequently communicate his experience through language:

> However, when these instinctual needs are not met, and the infant ego cannot find a soothing and calming mother, the mother's shadow, which is witch-like and related to destruction, death, and evil, colours the infant's experience. The infant feels persecuted by negative affects such as murderous rage and envy, which he needs to expel and dispose of outside of himself. (Sidoli, 2000, p. 74)

The mother's nurturing fosters the move from the concrete to the symbolic. But, if the infant's dependency needs are not met, intolerable "panic, anxiety, frustration, rage and murderous feelings" lead to the use of primitive defences of the self that "keep the infant isolated in the world of archetypal fantasies" (2000, p. 75). Sidoli hypothesises that this happens when primitive affects, brought about by certain experiences in infancy, were not attributed any psychic meaning by the mother, due to her emotional or physical absence (2000, p. 103).

Sidoli speculates that in somatisation "the two polarities of the archetypal experience have been split into two halves: the body and the psyche. The instinctual part has remained lodged in the body and the spiritual part has become an empty image" (2000, p. 104). Where this occurs, there is a lack of fantasy, and "the proto-images— as archaic proto-fantasy/bodily elements—. . . [remain] buried or encapsulated in the unconscious bodily pole of the archetype" (2000, pp. 107–108). Important for understanding how the body in action can be dissociated from the psyche in perversion, she concludes:

> that the psychosomatic patient uses his or her own body or bodily organs (instead of the mother's mind) as a container and signifier, as a kind of stage upon which psychic pain can be dramatized and eventually relieved. The body becomes the container of pain, undifferentiated but concretely visible because as such it is attended to and relieved by a mother who understands suffering only in concrete terms. There is no room for invisible, impalpable psychic pain. The somatic symptom becomes an expression, a dramatization of psychic pain which has the quality of a mime rather than a play. It is a drama without words, through which the body of the sufferer will receive the primary care that will vicariously provide solace and comfort to the soul. (Sidoli, 2000, p. 15)

Sidoli also connects the tendency to somatise with a lack in the development of the transcendent function (2000, p. 116), a function that Norah Moore (1983, p. 133) describes as a bridge, dependent for its development on the real world context of mother, mother–baby, and body. She regards symbols as body-based, related to body zones, and with bodily and spiritual aspects, akin to bi-polar archetypes.

Infant research generally confirms the significance of "an innate program of sensual-affectionate needs which plays a decisive and important role in the mother-infant relationship" (Jacoby, 1999, pp. 110–115). Like Kalsched, Sidoli, and Knox, Jacoby links early attachment problems to later psychosomatic disturbances. He suggests that due to problems of attachment, there may be a lack of integration of sex, sensuality, and affection in adulthood and that:

> Sexual complexes of various kinds usually serve as a symptomatic reflection of more generalized psychological disturbances; i.e. other motivational systems are also typically implicated. For example "voyeurism may be connected to the motivation of curious exploration and exhibitionism likened to the genuinely existential need to be seen, to experience "the gleam in mother's eyes" (Kohut), an essential way of self-confirmation. (Jacoby, 1999, p. 115)

One last aspect of somatisation mentioned by Sidoli (2000, p. 41), is the significance of repetition. In the learning process, repeated good experiences counteract repeated bad ones. However, the repetition of negative experiences, which constellate the negative aspect of the mother archetype, contribute to severe pathology, in which repetition as a compulsion can be used by the infant to defend against change, and ultimately against psychic growth. This fits with Verhaeghe's (2004, p. 316) understanding that addictive adults lack the ability to process psychologically and, through what he calls secondary processing, attempt to treat their psychological problems by intervening directly with their body through repetitive action. Repetition compulsion is illustrated in Chapter Seven as a defensive behavioural quality of perversion.

This section shows how infantile trauma may become an embodied symbol that could later be expressed vengefully as a perversion. It also indicates how damage to the transcendent function might be a precursor to splitting and projection, with conscious actions that appear to have no conscious meaning but have unconscious, including archetypal, significance.

Fourth conceptual difference: teleology and understanding of causation

At the beginning of his career, Jung is confined to the clinical evaluation of symptomatology within a mechanistic psychiatric model, but his intuitive mind eschews reductionism and scientific materialism. As his career progresses, he adopts a prospective view towards psychopathology, recognising both the positive value of symptoms and the symbolic expression they carry (Jung, 1914, pars. 438–465). He places less emphasis on repression, moving towards a Hegelian, hermeneutic approach that emphasises meaning rather than causality, the psychic disposition of the patient rather than childhood events, and the symbolic significance of behaviour and experience (Frey-Rohn, 1974, p. 195). Through philosophical idealism, he privileges depth of meaning above medical diagnosis, placing the psyche in a broad cultural and historical context with the individual inseparable from the collective. He adopts a philosophy of perspectivism, described by Hauke as "a metaphor of epistemology as *vision* . . . [as opposed to] the scientific objectivity of classical scientific empiricism . . ." (Hauke, 2000, p. 152). Reductionism is relegated to a subordinate position in theoretical understanding. Interpreted clinically,

"We reduce as part of deconstructing the image and metaphor in the service of integration and hence individuation, not in the service of causality" (Astor, 2002, pp. 604–605).

Jung describes causality as "a point of view" (Jung, 1916c, par. 687) and introduces the term "synchronicity" (Jung, 1951a, par. 969) to describe meaningful coincidence without obvious causal connection between unconscious products and external events. He believes that only the unconscious has a priori knowledge, usually in the form of images, associated with archetypal processes (Jung, 1928, par. 300). For Bright (1997, p. 633) this psychoid dimension to meaning underlies the analytic attitude and is Jung's modification of hermeneutics; his concept of the transcendent nature of meaning, a meaning that can be understood in archetypal terms (1997, p. 621) and implies universal interrelatedness.

Jung's interpretation of symptomatology develops towards a belief in the teleological directedness of everything psychic. "Anything psychic is Janus-faced—it looks both backwards and forwards. Because it is evolving, it is also preparing the future" (Jung, 1921, par. 718). He explains fixation as usually relating to ". . . the moment when a new psychological adjustment, that is, a new adaptation, is demanded" (Jung, 1916a, par. 563). Similarly, the regressive tendency is ". . . a genuine attempt to get at something necessary" in order to move forward (Jung, 1930, par. 55). This approach requires a refocusing from the past to the present. Freud's emphasis on what is remembered moves to Jung's focus on how it is currently remembered. Jones (2002, p. 47–48) explains teleology as a *futural* sense of time operating in the present and acting through the imagining of possibilities. Although not directly experienced, it carries the imprint of the collective unconscious. "Through teleology time's future becomes a symbol" (2002, p. 47). He is describing a backwards and forwards appreciation of temporal causation held in the present.

From this teleological perspective, Morgenthaler describes a symptom as "a creative attainment of the ego" (Morgenthaler, 1988, p. 12) and Hogenson (1994, p. 15) considers the telos of the organism to be its organisation and the fulfilment of the functions of its parts. Cowan regards pathologising as "one of the soul's characteristic activities" (Cowan, 1982, p. 5), true to the term psychopathology, a composite of meaning (logos), of suffering (pathos), and of the soul (psyche). She believes that "Through its 'psychopathologies', the soul speaks of its conditions, and perhaps its intentions, by means of symptoms, dreams, fantasies, and behaviour; it does so individually and collectively" (1982, p. 6).

Stevens and Price maintain that "Psychopathology results when the environment fails, either partially or totally, to meet one (or more) archetypal need(s) in the developing individual" (Stevens & Price, 1996, p. 34). Hillman has a similar perspective, using the term pathologising to mean "the psyche's autonomous ability to create illness, morbidity, disorder, abnormality, and suffering in any aspect of its behaviour and to experience and imagine life through this deformed and afflicted perspective" (Hillman, 1991b, p. 143). For him pathologising is seen as a way of mythologising, as the psyche reverts to a mythical style of consciousness to find another reality in which the pathologising makes sense (Hillman, 1991b, p. 146).

In perversion the futural sense is expressed at first through the psyche's creation of symptoms as opportunities for healing and movement towards health; a teleological directedness. This contrasts with the psycho-analytic understanding that perversion begins with misconception and denial (disavowal) at the outset. In my formulation, the psyche's *inability to use the curative value of the symptoms it creates* (intrapsychic relational projections), and to reintegrate projections, means that further defensive action is needed to protect the fragile and divided psyche. At this stage both the integrity and the development (telos) of the psyche is sacrificed to the need to strengthen and maintain defences for future protection, and incoming relational possibilities are perversely interpreted as ominous challenges. Other people are "dealt with" rather than "related to". This progression into severe psychopathology will be formulated in the following chapter.

CHAPTER SEVEN

Formulation including a Jungian perspective

O vengence

Shakespeare, *Hamlet*, Act 3: Scene 1

The theoretical formulation that follows includes Jungian concepts and ideas, situating perversion within a theoretical framework that can be understood from both a Jungian and a psycho-analytic perspective. My intention is to elucidate the psychic development of perversion, its dynamics, and the nature of its persistence. The theoretical formulation draws upon the Jungian ideas and concepts described in Chapter Six, as well as the psycho-analytic theory presented in Chapter Four. Additional concepts, not introduced previously, have been assigned and adapted from areas outside psychoanalysis where no established concept exactly covers a particular aspect of perversion.

Perversion is a function of the whole psychic system, including its historical and futural aspects, replicated in microcosm or macrocosm, with the detail representing the whole, in all perverse conceptions and expressions from ideation to perverse enactment. There is intricate psychic patterning with detail and whole echoing each other in an enfolding structure. Such complex structuring is typical of other systems, such as Bohm's implicate order (Bohm, 1883, p. 149); the fractal scaling of Mandelbrot's geometry (Briggs, 1992, p. 149); in Sheldrake's morphic resonance (Sheldrake, 1987, pp. 74–77); and in Piaget's innate schemata (Flavell, 1963, pp. 52–55). However, all these systems are natural, organic, and potentially self-enhancing, whereas the perverse structure lures and distorts, locking and linking experience into destructive processes.

Although the perverse structure is established initially through stage by stage progression, thereafter it consists of constellations of impulses, fantasies, anxieties, and defences that are all continuously present, whether latent or active, and capable of multiple duplication, twisting, turning, and enfolding (Parsons, 2000, p. 40). Similarly, the formulation is intended as a holistic and non-linear model, congruent with the functional aspects of the subject matter it addresses.

The four conceptual differences between psycho-analytic and Jungian theory discussed in the previous chapter are briefly re-presented below to indicate how the inclusion of a Jungian perspective offers new possibilities for a more comprehensive understanding of perversion, with sexual and non-sexual perversion positioned under the same conceptual umbrella.

1. Expansion of the understanding of the libido, including the replacement of "polymorphous perversity" with "polyvalent germinal disposition". This aids the perception of perversion as a relational, rather than an exclusively sexual, psychopathology.
2. Inherited instinctual processes are reinterpreted as archetypally structured *psychological* possibilities, linked with imagery and with perceptive ideas. This provides a framework for understanding the templating of relationships through a blinkered perception of others. A template dictates how a relationship is perceived and so determines the specific quality of relational behaviour and often defines an exact relational scenario of vengeful action.
3. Collective unconscious determinants that were never in personal consciousness structure the psyche and become embodied as relational metaphor. The transcendent function is stultified, attacking healthy and imaginative links between conscious and unconscious, archetypal myth and personal narrative. The inability to symbolise means that the remnants of personal myth representing

the state of the psyche, are overwhelmed by archetypal determinants. The perverse psychic structure employs extreme archetypal defences, functioning to protect the psyche (by attack) from perceived external threat. The focus on defensive processes is at the expense of psychic growth and development. The defence of regression, in its more severe form, moves psychic functioning back beyond the personal to an earlier evolutionary stage, through the employment of primitive cognitive structures.

4.   Teleology helps to explain how perversion starts with healthy defensive moves. The psyche's *creation* of symptoms reveals a futural sense, a teleological directedness towards healing and health, with the future directing the present. This process sours if it is not accompanied by movement towards psychic wholeness. Perversion, associated with splitting and dissociation, is one outcome of such failure in which the future is perceived as dangerous and menacing. Constantly anticipating psychic insult, the perverse psyche becomes proactive, turning past experiences of humiliation into a desire to victimise others.

The theoretical formulation takes account of the different theoretical positions introduced in Chapter Four, although it does not precisely follow any of them. As in the psycho-analytic model, I understand perversion as a deviation of either aim or object, although not necessarily a deviation from adult genital sexuality (Freud, 1905d, p. 165), but rather from its more general relational equivalent—whole person, empathic relationship. Although there is an assumption of early psychic insult or humiliation, this is not necessarily of a sexual nature. The perverse structure is seen as a defence against anxieties and conflicts that may not be Oedipal or even sexual (Freud, 1919e; Gillespie, 1956, p. 398; McDougall, 1972, p. 378; Verhaeghe, 2004, pp. 127–128). There is also identity confusion, (Bak, 1968, p. 16; McDougall, 1972, p. 375; Rangell, 1991, p. 17), although again not necessarily sexual. The defensive mechanisms employed are those of psycho-analysis; splitting (Gillespie, 1956, p. 402), denial in the form of disavowal (Freud, 1927e, p. 153), dissociation, idealisation, although not of the pregenital self (Chasseguet-Smirgel, 1974, p. 349) but of a narrowly prescribed relationship, and regression, but beyond personal infancy to an archaic earlier stage in which technique dominates the relationship. As in psycho-analysis, functioning of the perverse psychic structure is characterised by aggression and sadism culminating in triumph (Kernberg, 1988, p. 1007; Mawson, 1999, pp. 1 & 7; Stoller, 1977, pp. 96–101), by addiction and compulsion (Adler, 1986, p. 187; Kaplan, 1991, p. 10; Mawson, 1999, p. 6; McDougall, 1972, p. 372; Money, 1988; Steiner, 1993, p. 103–104;), and by rigidity (Coen, 1992, p. 224; Kaplan, 1991, p. 10; McDougall, 1972, p. 371; 1978, p. 198; Steiner, 1993, p. 27).

I make a different interpretation of the onset and operation of these defences, placing more emphasis on projection, which I describe in the formulation as a two stage process. Denial partly conforms to the psycho-analytic concept of disavowal, with simultaneous belief in conflicting objective and psychic realities, but the psycho-analytic concept of disavowal is traditionally sexual and prescribes a substitute sexual object choice, whereas in my formulation it is not the maternal phallus (or the mother) that is disavowed, but the image and affect of unbearable relationship. The substitute is not, nor does it represent, a body part, but it does represent the embodiment of infantile trauma. The relational image and affect is unconsciously reversed through an altered state of perception, so that in the ensuing perverse scenario the one who is humiliated becomes the humiliator.

I believe that the initial defensive manoeuvres in perversion can have positive value, acting as supportive adjuncts to healthy deintegrative / reintegrative processes, but if these manoeuvres fail, severe dissociative defences develop into a perverse core that dominates the psyche. This obstructs healthy development towards psychic sophistication, which is a process requiring connectedness through imaginative and symbolic thought. The formulation shows how the perverse psychic structure attacks the quality of human thought by oversimplification and debasement, and how human feeling becomes driven by the perverse psychic system for destructive ends, leaving no place for the understanding of others, for compassion, or for empathy. This dissociated state is theoretically represented in the creation and maintenance of an alternative psychic space, holding an oblique relationship to the central psychic organisation. As dissociation within the psyche is concealed through deception, including self-deception, interaction with others lacks positive human qualities, and can reflect little more than a deceptive, codified, statement of sadistic psychic intent.

Short extracts from, and references to, three biographies are used to illustrate consistent themes of perversion in the lives of the biographees as researched by the authors. Summaries of each biography are given next to indicate the stance taken by the biographers, none of whom set out to present a study of perversion. The summaries also demonstrate that the extracts selected for illustration are generally typical of the biographee as described in the biography.

Fred West—a case of sexual perversion

Biography—Happy Like Murderers by Gordon Burn (1998)

This is a joint biography of Fred West and his second wife (only Fred himself is considered here). West is presented as a deceptively friendly and likeable character. Beneath this persona he is cold, uncaring, violent, predatory, and scheming. The account of his life describes him as a serial killer who rapes, tortures, and murders at least a dozen young women in Gloucester in the 1970s including his first wife and one of his daughters. Sexually he is a voyeur who pimps his wife to watch her having sex with other men. He is not interested in their whole bodies, only their genitals. He sexualises everything. West is depicted as constantly active and agitated. When sexually active, he likes to be surrounded by his tools; when not sexually active he is preoccupied with the use of these tools. If not out at work, he is drilling, digging, and constructing in his own house. He makes holes in and under his house in which his dismembered victims are posted after the removal of trophy bones. The author describes no redeeming qualities, but throws light on West's perversion and violent sexual behaviour by relaying the popular understanding that he was physically abused as a child and sexually abused by both parents. At the age of nineteen he was charged with having regular sex with his thirteen-year-old sister and being the father of her baby.

Although West is better known as a serial killer, details of this biography are used to illustrate the development and establishment of his sexual perversion.

Dr Harold Shipman—a case of bodily perversion

Biography—Harold Shipman: Mind Set on Murder by Carole Peters (2005)

Harold Shipman is Britain's most prolific serial killer. His biography is written by a television producer with assistance from criminal profilers and access to the database of a four year public enquiry into Shipman's crimes which concluded that while a hospital doctor and then a GP he killed about 260 of his patients over a period of some thirty years. The author's account of Shipman's life is factual, offering what detail is available of the sequence of murders and the circumstances of each one. Peters describes Shipman's reputation as the best doctor in town, loved and admired by his patients, even at a time when he was killing several of them every month. She claims to be investigating why he killed, but does not provide any clear answers, other than factually highlighting the close relationship with his mother and the experience of her painful, protracted death from cancer when he was an adolescent. Shipman witnessed the GP's daily visits to administer morphine injections to his mother, which only partly alleviated her pain. The author believes that Shipman was addicted to killing, although the development of the addiction is not adequately explained, only the link between the circumstances of his mother's death and his consistent modus operandi of killing by lethal injection.

The author does not relate Shipman's behaviour to perversion. However, this biography is referenced to illustrate how the concept of perversion can be extended to include behaviour emanating from a perverse psychic structure where the behavioural focus is not essentially sexual but nevertheless is centred on the body.

Robert Maxwell—a case of emotional and cognitive perversion

Biography—Robert Maxwell: Israel's Superspy *by Gordon Thomas and Martin Dillon (2002)*

This is a comprehensively researched account of Maxwell's life from childhood to international publisher, politician, and industrialist. The first author, Gordon Thomas, has published forty-three books of both fiction and non-fiction, with sales exceeding forty-five million copies. His co-author is Martin Dillon, an authority on global terrorism and author of a number of non-fiction books on the subject. The book is primarily concerned with Maxwell's dealings out in the world, fuelled by his competitiveness and ruthless ambition. He is shown as constantly seeking to increase his wealth, power, and influence, often through exploitation and mendacity. His double-dealing ultimately back-fires as the plotter is plotted against. In seeking at least \$400 million to stave off his creditors, Maxwell unknowingly engineers the downfall of his empire and his own assassination. Maxwell as presented in this biography, exemplifies neither sexual nor bodily perversion, although if both cognition and emotion are perversely geared towards perverse ends, every aspect of life is tainted. If, as might perhaps be argued, there is some suggestion of either sexual or bodily perversion in this biography, this is clearly governed by cognitive and emotional perverse functioning and entirely subsidiary to it rather than an end in itself.

This biography is used to illustrate how the concept of perversion can be extended to include the manifestations of emotional and cognitive perversion emanating from a perverse psychic structure, shown through mendacity and deception. The biographee, as depicted, demonstrates many of the characteristics of the trickster archetype.

Theoretical formulation

My theoretical formulation will be presented as sequential statements, from A through to I, with explanatory text following each stage. Accompanying every statement, brief biographical material from each of the three cases will be presented as illustration. Finally, the statements will be combined at the end of the chapter to give a complete exposition of the conceptual model.

A. The predisposition to perversion presumes a conjunctive affective memory of unbearable relational experience

"Conjunction memory" is a term chosen by the neuroscientists Olson, Page, Moore, Chatterjee, and Verfaellie (2006, pp. 4596–4601) to describe the memory of relationship between two stimuli, as distinct from the "feature memory" of a single stimulus. I have used the adjectival form "conjunctive" to describe an often indelible memory of trauma in relationship. Such conjunctive memories are associative, linking together people, objects, and scenes with images, feelings, and sensations. Bound together, they form an affective symbol of the relational quality at the time of the trauma rather than an accurate memory of events (Van der Kolk & Fisler, 1996, p. 353).

Nissan (2007, p. 418) describes the establishment of such memory impressions. He conceives of memory as a reconstructive process with the goal of making sense of experience rather than remembering it exactly as it occurred. "It would be reasonable for our memory to endorse inaccurate or false interpretations of events, if these interpretations would assist us in making sense of our experience" (2007, p. 418). He describes the capacity to "gist" (2007, p. 418) in achieving this goal, which is the ability to put things into a semantic context to create an appropriate framework for them. Although his emphasis is on linguistics, he suggests that false associations might be established through gisting, and that feeling equivalence could lead to memory confusion. Such sustained memory impressions combined with feeling equivalence play an influential role in my theoretical formulation.

An experience is unbearable if it cannot be carried by the psychic structure in an initial step towards integration. Such an experience is regarded as traumatic if it is also overloaded with negative affect. Mogenson describes such traumatic experience as "overwhelming" and generally "outside the available parameters of experience" since there is an insufficient field of comparison. "A traumatic event is not pushed out of awareness; rather, it is too big to register in awareness" (Mogenson, 2005, p. 87).

Research suggests that it is not just one traumatic incident that causes catastrophic disequilibrium: cumulative trauma, neglect, and carer disengagement might be equally debilitating (Schore, 2003, pp. 180–187). This concurs with Kernberg's diagnostic criteria for severe personality disorders (Kernberg, 1984, pp. 3–26) associated with traumatic experiences, such as physical or sexual abuse, severe deprivation of love, severe neglect, and unavailable parental objects. This wider area of trauma causation leads to recognition that some damaging traumata may be more subtle than once thought and not necessarily intrusive. (The idea of less detectable, but never-the-less powerfully influential, infantile trauma would be congruent with the work of chaologists who reveal that dynamical systems, that might include the psyche, exhibit extreme sensitivity to initial conditions (Briggs, 1992, p. 18).

A relational perspective on trauma is considered essential to the understanding of perversion, since perverse symptomatology is expressed through relationship with others. Perhaps the most prominent characteristic of the perverse internal and external relationship is inequality, which, coupled with lack of empathy, means the exploitation of one party by the other. Buber (2000, pp. 23–24) distinguishes this kind of "I–it" relationship in which the invented other is used and abused and given the characteristics of a transitional object, from an "I–thou" relationship in which the other is perceived as a whole person.

Stevens indicates how the understanding of later relationships is templated by infantile experience: ". . . as the child experiences the mother so, by analogy and extension, he experiences life and the world" (Stevens, 2002, p. 120). Mogenson (2005, p. 80) extends the familial metaphor to whatever traumatises us transferentially *becomes* our parent or, in reverse, we are infantilised by whatever we cannot master. It then follows that "a failure of fit" (2005, p. 83) between the world and the world as anticipated by the psyche, (Bion's mating of mind and matter), "backfires into what Jung called "incest"" and impingements of the self feel like incestuous abuse and we feel "raped by what [our parents] did or did not do to us" (2005, p. 83).

Case One—Fred West— as presented by Gordon Burn
(Burn, 1998)—sexual perversion

West was raised in an atmosphere of sexual exploitation. Incest, sexual and physical abuse, and humiliation were rife within the family. His father's attitude was, "If it's on offer, take it". His father took it for granted that it was his right to begin his daughters' sexual life. "Your first baby should be your Dad's" (Burn, 1998, p. 141). Rumour had it that West was sexually abused by his father, having lost his virginity to his mother when he was twelve. West's sexual experiences from a young age would have been impossible for his immature psyche to integrate and might be assumed to have left unbearable memories of inappropriate sexual intimacy, intrusion and attack.

Case Two—Harold Shipman—as presented by Carole Peters
(Peters, 2005)—bodily perversion

Shipman had a powerful and doting mother to whom he was strongly attached. In the last stage of her life she suffered from lung cancer, and Shipman was oppressed by her unavailability and her preoccupation with extreme bodily pain that was only alleviated through daily doses of morphine. Shipman was usually present when the doctor administered

the morphine (Peters, p. 120). His powerlessness to ease her pain or to
prevent her death when he was aged seventeen is likely to have been a
humiliating experience leaving an indelible scar.

Case Three—Robert Maxwell—as presented by
Gordon Thomas and Martin Dillon
(Thomas & Dillon, 2002)—emotional and cognitive perversion

There is no suggestion of either sexual or physical abuse in Maxwell's
early life. He came from a large and desperately poor orthodox Jewish
family living in "a remote corner of what became Czechoslovakia" that
had the bloodstain of a violent history of anti-Semitism (Thomas & Dillon,
2002, pp. 16–17). Maxwell walked barefoot in summer and shared shoes
with his siblings in winter (p. 26). He had a particularly close relationship
with his mother who was intelligent and well informed, different from
other local women. She was both a political activist and a Zionist and
picked up every piece of newspaper in the street to discover what was
going on (p. 21). She warned her son that he would have to leave the
village and make his own way in the world. So he left home at sixteen
(p. 22) and never returned to his family. Within six years he had lost both
parents, his grandfather, three sisters, and a brother, as well as aunts,
uncles, and other relatives, in the Holocaust, mostly at Auschwitz.

B. Initially, the same defensive mechanisms of splitting and projection are used as in non-perverse development, with temporary removal of unintegrated relational material in the form of a psychic sticker, associated with one or more complexes, so that it may be deconstructed and imbued with new meaning

I have introduced the new concept of *psychic sticker* as it offers a
clearer theoretical conceptualisation of how perverse processes are
initiated than any existing term. *Psychic sticker* refers to the projected
psychic representation in microcosm of the image and affect associated with unbearable relationship. It differs from a splinter psyche or
subpersonality (Chapter Six: Complexes) in that its qualities and
concerns are strictly relational. The word *sticker* is specifically chosen
as communicating the idea of temporarily projected content that
requires attention. (*The Oxford English Dictionary* (1989) defines a
sticker as "an adhesive label, a small adhesive notice designed to be

stuck in a conspicuous place"). Initially the sticker is an animated projection, animated in the sense of containing unrecognised otherness (Jung, 1929b, par. 55). It is an affective image with imperative, magnetic, and emblematic power that arises as a reaction to an overburdening demand for receptivity in the psyche. When the psyche is unable sufficiently to expand in complexity to accommodate a new or traumatic experience, it may create a sticker. This can be a facility for psychic containment, protecting the ego from becoming overwhelmed by the archetypal power of traumatic experience. It is a signal of both separateness and connection that, when projected, absolves the psyche from responsibility for failure of accommodation. But in publicising itself to the psyche, it acts also as a reminder, flagging up a need to address the issue of its separateness.

So far the process described is not perverse. The creation of a psychic sticker is a forward-looking defensive operation intended to facilitate healthy developmental processes. Verghaeghe (2004, p. 317) makes the important observation for teleological understanding of this process and its consequences, that not only psychological disturbances, but all development begins with structural trauma, suggesting trauma can offer opportunities for development if the psyche is able to harness it effectively. But in order to take advantage of the opportunity that the sticker presents, there must be adequate psychic strength, sufficient to tolerate uncertainty, contemplate change, and consider new ways of perceiving both oneself and others in relationship. Since perversion is a defensive, rather than a progressive development, it is unlikely to emerge from a robustly functioning psyche.

Perversion implies the desperate hanging on to the known as an implicit belief, rather than making use of the sticker, entering into dialogue with it, playing with alternative possibilities, perspectives, and truths.

Case One—Fred West—sexual perversion

The theme of dissociated sexuality and sexual preoccupation is found throughout West's biography. His first arrest was for shoplifting "women's items" when he was nineteen (Burn, 1998, p. 146). Reflecting his own premature sexualisation, sexual abuse, and experience of violence, West showed no respect for bodily privacy: there were no locks on the bathroom and toilet doors in his family house, which also accommodated lodgers (p. 61). He continued "His liking for smut. He liked talking about sex . . . He brought every conversation round to sex in the end" (p. 59). "He was obsessed with sex. He could never get away from sex. He saw sex in everything" (p. 241). "If he couldn't think about sex he couldn't think at all" (p. 272).

Case Two—Harold Shipman—bodily perversion

Shipman's affective memories of a close relationship with his mother as a living human being appear lost in the image of himself with her in death. It is this psychic sticker, a microcosm of distorted memory that he separated and held at a distance but without escaping its influence. At medical school he showed an unusual fascination with corpses (Peters, 2005, p. 125).

Case Three—Robert Maxwell—emotional and cognitive perversion

Superficially, Maxwell led the life of one whose success was grounded in work and astute financial judgment. But he demonstrated the use of psychic stickers as he inhabited a separate world (of deception and mendacity) of which he outwardly claimed no part. In this other world he lived the fantasy of his mother's dream, "If you are ambitious there is nothing that is impossible" (Thomas & Dillon, 2002, p. 21). He could alter his identity with a change of name. He dropped the name Abraham to be less Jewish (p. 21), then following his mother's wish that he should become an Englishman he called himself du Maurier after a cigarette popular with the English middle and upper classes, then Leslie Jones. When promoted at the age of twenty-one to second lieutenant in the British army he changed his name again to Ian Robert Maxwell (p. 26). He now had the unintegrated accoutrements of an officer and a gentleman.

C. The work required for healthy development is that the psyche address the projected imagery and affect on all levels of consciousness, and also as its own experience of the external world

I will discuss this stage at length as it represents a key turning point towards or away from perversion. Movements out from the centre of the self, to create other centres through projective processes, are a familiar form of defence, and teleologically could be regarded as a healthy deintegrative attempt to separate psychic input that cannot immediately be processed, giving the psyche opportunities to deal with it away from other psychic concerns. If temporary, this division of the self could be seen as a positive development, creating a place for "psychic homework", or private reiteration and consideration of experiences that were at first unacceptably difficult to integrate because of their magnitude, strangeness, or suddenness.

A sticker puts the psyche "on the spot", forcing an unconscious decision as to whether, when, and how the relationship issues represented by the sticker are to be addressed. Much will depend on the psyche's ability to use the transcendent function, making links between the real and the imaginary, the rational and irrational, consciousness and the unconscious (Chapter Six: Symbolisation and the transcendent function). Moving into the space and depth of this reflective function requires the capacity to conceive of the conscious and unconscious states of both self and other in the relational adversity represented by the sticker.

Working on a psychic sticker to assist the process of integration is an emotional, more than a cognitive, process. The psyche needs to integrate the dissociated material into its own narrative or myth, tapping the archetypal disposition to order personal experience. Both conscious and unconscious imaginative processes need to work cooperatively, to deconstruct, reconstruct, and understand in different ways and from various perspectives. Imagination is described by Eisner (2002, p. 5) as a form of thinking that engenders images of the possible, enabling us to try things out in the mind's eye, without the possible consequences of acting on them empirically. As Eisner (2002, p. 6) states, "Representation can and often does begin with an elusive and sometimes evanescent idea or image . . . representation stabilizes the idea or image . . . and makes possible a dialogue with it". In these terms it becomes a projective inscription that can be related to and worked upon. He describes inscribing, editing, and communicating as the three cognitive processes used in the act of representation. Imagery also has the function described by Money-Kyrle (1971, p. 105; see also Chapter Six: Image) of presenting to the mind a preconcept, just able to be a thought, without being fully conceptualisable as an idea.

At this deeper imaginative level, Gordon describes how archetypal experiences or images, motifs and forms "enliven and enrich"

(Gordon [1983–1984], p. 23) the inner world, with imaginative recombination and patterning, involving symbolisation or the transcendent function (Chapter Six: Symbolisation and the transcendent function). She cites Plaut's (1966) observation that the "capacity to imagine constructively is closely related to, if not identical with the capacity to trust" (Gordon, 1993, p. 131). This would make imagination particularly difficult for those suffering from perversions, whose trust in carers may have been betrayed.

The building up of trust-related imaginative capabilities, leading to the ability to symbolise, relates to all three stages of the formulation presented so far. Gordon ([1983–1984], p. 16) describes the infantile antecedents to this humanising capacity. Emerging from the unconscious, archetypal images and affects are first experienced only through projection and identification as if they belonged to the outside world and "the infant tends to perceive himself and the people around him as essentially *in*human or *non*human" (Gordon, 1993, p. 22). This early state is followed by a gradual differentiation of self and not-self. At the same time objects in the non-self world are beginning to separate from each other rather than being perceived as part-objects linked to other part-objects by affect. When this is achieved, Winnicott's third area evolves, developing out of experience of the transitional object and capable of symbol-making and, importantly for perverse dynamics, capable of an "as-if" attitude that allows for representation without identification. Gordon ([1983–1984], p. 15) describes the development of this third area of not quite inner or outer, but dependent upon reaching the depressive position, or Winnicott's "stage of concern", when the ego is sufficiently robust to distinguish inner and outer, psyche and soma, self from other, and to hold trust in constancy and continuity. She comments on the close similarity between Winnicott's concept of the third, the area of experience and illusion, and Jung's description of a place or medium of realisation that "is neither mind nor matter but that *intermediate realm of subtle reality* which can only be adequately expressed by the symbol. The symbol is neither abstract nor concrete, neither rational nor irrational, neither real nor unreal. It is always both" (Gordon, 1993, p. 19).

A traumatised person, or someone who has not developed an adequate sense of self in relation to others, will find it difficult to look reflectively inwards. Although not specifically considering personal relationships, this ability is named by Senge, Scharmer, Jaworski, and

Flowers as "presencing", meaning having the time to sense, become one with the world, and retreat down to where inner knowledge can emerge. It is a state of becoming totally present to the larger space or field and to an expanded sense of self. Getting in touch with what is emerging precedes realisation and action. (Senge, Scharmer, Jaworski, & Flowers, 2005, pp. 86 & 91). Presencing is teleological through not being over-dependent on the past, which might give inaccurate guidance, but ". . . seeing beyond external reality and beyond even seeing from within the living whole. It is seeing from within the source from which the future whole is emerging, peering back at the present from the future" (Senge, Scharmer, Jaworski, & Flowers, 2005, pp. 90–91).

The work of Claxton provides a perspective for comparing the resourcefulness of being able to stop and use the reflective function with the sort of part-mind thinking that leads to precipitous action in perversion. He conceives of the mind as possessing three different processing speeds (Claxton, 1998, pp. 1–2). The first, necessary and appropriate in some situations, is our "wits" (1998, p. 2), this is faster than thought and involves instantaneous and unselfconscious reaction. The second is the speed of thought itself, employed in working things out, assessment of situations, weighing up alternatives, and solving problems. These two stages are also identified by West (2007, p. 13) who cites Ohman's (1986) studies to demonstrate two dissociable modes of processing affective information, a rapid, unconscious, pre-attentive analysis of an emotional stimulus followed by a later conscious assessment of the relevance of the same emotional stimulus. Claxton calls this second stage of intellectual involvement the "d" mode, denoting "deliberation". Third, he identifies the "tortoise mind" (as opposed to "the hare brain"), a slower process of "ruminating or mulling things over", a mode involving contemplation and meditation, "pondering over a problem rather than earnestly trying to solve it". He argues that "allowing the mind to meander" is not a luxury but a "vital part of the cognitive armamentarium" (Claxton, 1998, p. 2). This slower speed permits the appreciation of subtle patterns and delicate complexities (Claxton, 1998, p. 4) and the application of wisdom rather than intellect, since it requires tolerating confusion and uncertainty, assuaging anxiety, and forming an alliance between reason and intuition (Claxton, 1998, pp. 6–8 & 75). Claxton understands the creative mind as possessing a dynamic integrated balance between deliberation and contemplation (Claxton, 1998, p. 96); between the discrete reasoning processes of causalism to synchronicity and an inner knowledge of universal interconnectedness. The ability to move between Claxton's processing speeds, without over-reliance on fast directed thought, offers the best chance of rendering the psychic sticker comprehensible and allowing it to be reintegrated.

Cases One, Two, and Three

> This process involves a turning inward, giving time for contemplation and reflection, rather than a turning away from the inner world in a drive towards action. Illustrations in the three biographies are significantly absent. It could be argued that all three biographers were less interested in the inner worlds of their biographees than in their behaviour, however all chose to write about people who were behaviourally extreme and attempted to convey an understanding of their subject to the reader. Despite this, there is no evidence given of West, Shipman, or Maxwell engaging effectively in this inner activity or of placing significant value upon it. One might assume that, at best, it was intermittent for all of them and not regarded as a personal inner resource to access at times of psychic conflict. There is some clear evidence of this process not taking place in the case of Shipman. Unlike the other two, Shipman's trauma focuses on one particular period in his life, the protracted death of his mother, and so the behaviour immediately following her death can be considered as communicating something of his state of mind. His first reaction, although it was a dark and wet night, was to go out for a long run, covering at least ten miles. He returned to school as normal on the Monday following her death, not mentioning the event until questioned, when he referred to it quite casually (Peters, 2005, p. 122). This behaviour suggests significant dissociation and denial with a lack of ability to address his feelings or turn to others to help him integrate his grief and loss.

D. If this process is successful and the material represented by the sticker is sufficiently reintegrated, use of the sticker can be relinquished and further defensive manoeuvres abandoned

The unconscious projection of stickers away from the central psychic system gives "time out" from conscious psychic functioning. The allowance of hesitation, repetition, and deviation (identified in the Radio Four panel game "Just a Minute" as the dysfunctions most difficult to avoid when "hare brain" speed and focus are demanded), provides opportunities for reintegration of the sticker. It can therefore be seen as a positive, developmental move on the part of the psyche. The risk is that reintegration may not easily be achieved, particularly if ego functioning is weak, and anxiety and suffering diminish the ability to deal with psychic conflict, to promote prospective functioning, or to envisage mutually rewarding relationships.

If this process is successful, through change in either the sticker or the accommodating psychic structure, the projected sticker gains a "good enough" psychic context to be reintegratable, and no longer poses a threat to the psyche requiring defensive action. The sticker and its allure have then usefully served their ephemeral function and the sticker loses its independent identity.

Cases One, Two, and Three

Since perverse defensive manoeuvres continue throughout each biography, it can be assumed that a sufficient level of integration is not achieved in any of the three cases and that psychic stickers remain dissociated from the main psychic system.

E. Perversion presumes a failure of this reintegrative process due to either inadequate processing of the projected contents or failure of the ejecting psychic system to develop schemata that can accommodate the projection

Splitting and projection may be used as positive functions, aiming towards eventual psychic change through processing, development, and reintegration. Neither sticker nor sticking is pathological, but the inability to reintegrate the sticker is a pathological development possibly heralding movement towards perversion. The threat to psychic cohesion occurs if the sticker is not worked on effectively enough to be brought back and reintegrated into the central psychic system, either because the psyche is unable to create a comparable field of events in which the unacceptable may be experienced as acceptable (Mogenson, 2005, p. 87), or because "psychic homework" fails to render the split off contents integratable.

Structural damage in the psyche (Ware, 1995, p. 8) may impede reintegrative capacity, as may weakness of the ego. Without sufficient ego strength, the archetypal may be overwhelming, take possession of ego functioning, and dominate relationships, rather than act in partnership with consciousness (Gordon [1983–1984], p. 21). The (out)rage initiating the projection fuels dissociation and, if severe, militates against a positive outcome. This is particularly so if the projected contents were always unconscious. Lack of creative imagination or intrapsychic connectedness in the "theatre" of the mind (Neumann, 1954, p. xxiv) indicates weak functioning of the transcendent function, which bridges conscious and unconscious, the personal and the transpersonal, inner and outer (Chapter Six: Symbolisation and the transcendent function). Defensive strategies may not allow time and space for the growth of psychic networking (Knox, 2004, pp. 64–65) involving the reassuring connectivity of the transcendent function. Fear and incomprehension may cause the psyche to take flight from the complexities of "irreconcilable meanings and unresolvable contradictions" (Savitz, 1990, p. 57). The period of time before this occurs could be thought of in ethological terms as a critical period in which a fight or flight decision is made unconsciously and dictates subsequent action (Burkhardt, 2005).

There is a two stage inadequacy in the failing process, initially through the inability of the centralised organising system to integrate the experience, which is then split off, and subsequently in the inability to reintegrate the separated sticker. Intrapsychic rivalry may occur at this second stage if the new centre musters psychic resources to support its own independent development rather than moving towards integration. Jung expresses such destructive separation alchemically through symbols of death, mutilation, and poisoning; with re-assimilation offering transformation from putrefaction to sweetness (Edinger, 1994, pp. 71–72; Jung, 1946, par. 472).

The psyche does not always make the "right decision" for itself since, as Schulz (2010, pp. 120–123) points out, being mistaken is part of being human. We draw "sweeping conclusions" (2010, p. 120) from our own experiences, weighting this personal evidence heavily in our judgements rather than taking account of a fuller range of evidence. Although discussing error rather than perversion, Schulz makes the very useful point that "although small amounts of evidence are sufficient to make us draw conclusions, they are seldom sufficient to make us revise them" (Schulz, 2010, p. 124). She suggests that we are looking for verification rather than falsification and therefore we are reluctant to abandon or revise our conceptual framework. "Remembering to attend to counterevidence isn't difficult; it is simply a habit of mind, it requires conscious cultivation" (2010, p. 132). Of course, a defensive frame of mind does not facilitate openness to conflicting viewpoints even if a lack of open-mindedness may mean that we are duped by the mismatch between reality and belief. In this connection Schulz also addresses the issue of dependence. Believing what someone close to us believes, protects us from the independent thought of admitting that we may have been deceived, perhaps by someone we love, such as a parent. It is helpful in understanding such a choice to refer to Matte Blanco's principle of symmetry in unconscious logic. According to this principle, asymmetrical relations are treated by the unconscious as if they were symmetrical (Matte Blanco, 1975, p. 38). Specifically, if the child's rejection of the parent is unconsciously equivalent to the parent's rejection of the child, turning from the ideas and beliefs of one's parent may be equivalent to the unbearable loss of parental love. But Schulz (2010, pp. 139–143) also points out that if the person we depend on does not, or cannot, protect us, we may turn to our own experience and depend on that instead. This is consistent with Kalsched's self-care system (Chapter Six: Defences), established through mistrust of others and subsequent avoidance of dependency upon them.

Case One—Fred West—sexual perversion

No evidence is given of West changing in his attitude towards himself or towards his abusive sexual experiences. The direction of his life remained unaltered, dominated by his sexually traumatic and chaotic past. While presenting as a hard working, likable, and friendly man, he had another life in which all his experiences were sexually tainted (Burn, 1998, pp. 59, 121, 127–128).

Case Two—Harold Shipman—bodily perversion

Shipman's attitude suggests that he remained unable to express his feelings or integrate the experiences that surrounded the death of his mother. A friend at school described him as ". . . a man of few words, a man of action, very determined, hard and quick; he had a real streak of ruthlessness" (Peters, 2005, p. 119). The unintegrated sticker inspired action rather than reflection. As a doctor, he was popular amongst colleagues and patients because of his hard work and had the reputation of "the best doctor in the town" (p. 22). Ironically, this was largely because of his unprofessionalism as he led a life dominated by his unconscious need to malevolently "attend to" the sick and experience them as the dying.

Case Three—Robert Maxwell—emotional and cognitive perversion

The biography depicts Maxwell as someone who never integrated the experiences of deprivation and overwhelming loss in his childhood and adolescence and so became dominated by them. Throughout his life he defensively compensated by greed and an "obsessive need for selfaggrandisement" (Thomas & Dillon, 2002, p. 21). Rather than risk feelings of being the insignificant and socially unvalued little person of his childhood, he focussed on a dream "to become one of the best-known faces in the world" (p. 32). This gave him a need for secrecy while courting publicity (p. 44).

F. If the sticker remains unintegrated, the projected contents can dissociate further and develop as a semi-independent ectype, a subcentre representing the form or idea of perverse relationship

The allure of the sticker may be such that the psyche is seduced into investment in the sticker as a preferred psychic centre, offering false hope of an existence devoid of anxiety and conflict. This denies the sticker's subordinate role in the psychic system: conflict between the sticker and the main psychic system is not addressed, so the person is "stuck" or "glued down" in a partial world. A second meaning of the word sticker now comes into play, "something which causes a person to stick or to be at a nonplus" or "a poser" (*OED*, 1989). Hogensen refers to fantasy as "the glue holding reality and the psyche together" (Hogensen, 1994, p. 132); in this case the glue holds only part of the psyche to part of reality leading to a gravely distorted perception.

With this development, the sticker becomes a subcentre, the reintegrative process fails and the projection remains dissociated. The dissociated sticker, representing perverse relationship, then claims congruence with the self, whilst actually rivalling it for psychic dominance. The sticker that once represented an unconscious hypothesis, no longer seeks confirmation from the psyche's unconscious theoretical data base, but begins to establish itself as an alternative system of verification through which all future feelings about relationships will be processed. The world thereby created is one of magical realism in which a false type of self-care is substituted for attachment to others. This internal process relates to the broader definitions of perversion in Chapter Three, including turning, turning the wrong way, and turning aside (Ayto, 1990, p. 557; *OED*, 1989, p. 619; Partridge, 1958, p. 771). The psyche's integrity is now threatened by the possibility of a new centre, offering protection but rejecting development towards individuation.

A second concept, not normally used psychologically but appearing in Islamic sacred geometry, is introduced to describe the status of the psychic sticker once it is dissociated to the extent of creating a separate subcentre working in opposition to integrative processes. A new term is necessary as there is not an existing concept that accurately describes the dominant, conjunctive, or relational image and affect that began as a psychic sticker and, if the process towards perversion continues, firms up as a more permanent form or idea of perverse relationship. When the subcentre that was once a psychic sticker loses its temporary ambivalent status, it will be referred to as an *ectype*. (Ectypography is a mode of etching. The word ectype refers to a copy, as opposed to an archetype or prototype, and derives from the Greek ek = from, and typos = stamp (Lawlor, 1982, pp. 6–7)). The rationale for introducing another new term is, as with psychic sticker, the lack of an existing name for a relational projection, and also the need to distinguish the temporary sticker from this more permanent and dangerous projection. Lawlor (1982) uses the term in sacred geometry, placing "ectypal" on a level between "typal" and "archetypal". He describes the archetypal as concerned with universal processes or dynamic patterns that can be considered independently of any structure or material form. On the next level (in his model he moves down from the archetypal) is the ectypal, which is the idea or form (in this case the idea or form is "perverse relationship"). At this level there is a structure but it is unmanifest, pure and formal. The next level is "typal", and would refer in the case of perversion, to a specific type of perverse expression, for example, exhibitionism, or necrophilia. The facility with which perversions can be classified typally without geographical or historical exemptions (e.g., exhibitionism, frotteurism), reflects archetypal organisation in the collective unconscious. At an archetypal level, individuals share perceptual predispositions with archetypal motifs ordering experience into typical patterns (Jung, 1928/31, par. 719). This is clearly demonstrated in sexually perverse enactments.

These three levels, or incorporating concepts, conform to the nesting principle advanced by Jones (2002, p. 49), who conceptualises a generational model of nested levels of filiation, each fitting into or round the next. This reflects the core structure of perversion, with perverse behavioural enactment nested in perverse relational ideation and affect, itself nested in the perverse psychic structure. Briggs (1992, p. 34) indicates that there is support from the field of neurology for this model of psychic serial containment as fractal rhythms and distinct fractal signatures have been found in dopamine and serotonin receptors in the brain, and in enzymes.

The development from psychic sticker to ectype represents a movement away from the cooperative use of psychic resources in the long-term pursuit of unity and wholeness. Instead, available resources are used defensively for future proofing the psyche against the worst possible outcome—psychic disintegration. Paradoxically, the integrity of the psyche is then compromised and the process of individuation is subverted.

The ectype could be thought of as a symbol, with all the positive and life-enhancing connotations this might imply (Chapter Six: Symbolisation and the transcendent function). It is certainly uniquely representative of a truth about traumatic conjunctive memory, yet it is falsely true in its relationship to the psyche as a whole. The ectype might more accurately be regarded as the shadow of a symbol, since its attraction and perfidious influence guide the psyche into a developmental cul-de-sac. Through attacks on meaning, and perversion of the networking and integrating possibilities of the transcendent function, the bamboozled psyche is lured into a Faustian pact, with the promise of an escape it cannot make along a path on which it may not return.

Case One—Fred West—sexual perversion

In the case of sexual perversion, the ectype, or form of relationship, refers to the imposition of sexuality upon a relationship. His sexuality was combined with violence. When he was a young man, eight violent assaults on girls and young women at the caravan site where he lived were attributed to West (Burn, 1998, p. 170) and he married a woman who also liked violent sex (p. 105). He was brought up on a farm (p. 135–138) which formed an inner reference for him to draw on for human breeding and killing. He confused people with animals. His pet name for his wife was "cow". "He constantly referred to her as his cow . . . He was always talking about wanting to put her with a bull" (p. 159).

West consistently projected sexual feelings onto tools which he always wanted around him when engaged in sex and which became fetishistic in the sense that the tools were essential for sexual satisfaction and were more significant than people. He particularly liked to have sex in his van where he kept most of his tools (pp. 125 & 147).

Case Two—Harold Shipman—bodily perversion

Following the traumatic and unintegrated experience of his powerlessness in the relationship with his mother at the time of her illness and death, the ectype resonating for Shipman related to death and the idea of power over life and death. Although his activities were not obviously sexual, the forensic psychologist Paul Britton associates the high of killing with sexual thrills but thinks that Shipman might have moved in the direction of gaining sexual pleasure from no contact at all beyond being close to a body, "so that fulfilment is entirely a cerebral and mental experience with no physical contact at all necessary" (Peters, 2005, p. 140).

Case Three—Robert Maxwell—emotional and cognitive perversion

The ectype influencing Maxwell's life, as depicted, might be summarised verbally as "dominance through wealth, self-promotion, and surveillance"—watch and be watched. This ectype concerns neither sexual nor bodily relationship since these, although difficult to exclude from the broad compass of the ectype, are not its focus. Maxwell became one of "the wealthiest men on earth" (Thomas & Dillon, 2002, p. 124) as well as one of "the world's leading media moguls" (p. 171). His profits of seventy-nine million dollars in 1985 "multiplied in five years by a staggering twenty times" (p. 124). His newspapers filled pages with the predictions of his future wealth (124). He encouraged every facet of his lifestyle to be photographed and chronicled (p. 6) and spent "a king's ransom on having every newspaper, television and radio station on earth monitored for any mention of him" (p. 6). "His £2 million penthouse in the heart of London was marble-floored with ceilings supported by Doric columns, which he said came from ancient Egypt . . . The truth was that the columns were hollow fakes" (pp. 6–7). At the time of conducting business with the country he wore a self-styled T-shirt bearing the emblazoned words "King of Bulgaria" (p. 82) and when travelling from Le Bourget airport, like heads of state, he would attach "a flashing blue light on the roof" of his car (p. 157).

Yet insecurity over his own position led him to bug the offices of his own staff. "Bugs were hidden behind wall panels, in light fittings, in the handsets of phones, in restrooms" (p. 125).

G. The perverse dynamics of the dissociated ectype threaten the integrity of the psychic system and command the employment of further defences. Projective defences are strengthened so that the relational content of the ectype is contextualised and becomes typal, producing a specific unconscious conviction which templates all relationships and is underpinned by the vengeful projection of a kleptocracy as a whole world view of relationships

Perversion now conforms to one definition given in Chapter Three, "to subvert, put down or confute" (Adair, 1993, p. 86); it also has the taint of evil (Dollimore, 1991, pp. 124 & 147). By this stage perversion becomes established as an opponent of the process of individuation and development towards wholeness. Gordon (1993, p. 19) describes two fundamental tendencies in individuation, movement towards separation and differentiation, offering fragments of the unconscious to the processes of consciousness, and a counter movement toward unity of what has been separated and differentiated, a tendency Neumann calls "centroversion" (1954, p. 37). The balance is governed at all levels behind the scenes by an archetypal author/director/actor/managership (Stevens, 2002, p. 59). By definition, perversion does not conform to the controls of this balancing and counterbalancing system aimed at achieving psychic unity; its dynamic is not oppositional (regulatory) but distorting and dissociative. Perversion is about loss of the Way of individuation (N. Moore, 1983, pp. 120–121) with its balance of deintegrative and reintegrative capacities (Astor, 1995, pp. 128–129 & 237–238). The ectype takes control of the psyche, exerting "undue influence" (Martin, 2003, pp. 365–366), a legal use of the term perversion described in Chapter Three, with domination of the healthy by the unhealthy part of the personality (Steiner, 1982, p. 250; see also Chapter Four: Narcissism).

Once the sticker becomes established as an ectype, a personal myth is established (Chapter Six: Myth, metaphor, and narrative) through intrapsychic dictatorship, and the form of projected relationship hyperbolically infuses the whole personality with sadistic (Chasseguet-Smirgel, 1985; Freud, 1905d; Gillespie, 1940; Greenacre, 1996; Mawson, 1999; Parsons, 2000) and destructive motives, creating a new unconscious order. The hope of re-establishing democracy may then be greatly reduced and perhaps only achievable through psychotherapeutic means (Redfearn, 1992, p. 259–260). There is now a loss of free will (Dollimore, 1991, p. 124; McDougall, 1972, p. 371).

While the perception of a kleptocracy might be viewed as a fictive error, or psycho-analytically as a delusion, the Jungian view would be to regard it as a psychic reality. As Jung states, "The psychic alone has immediate reality, and this includes all forms of the psychic, even 'unreal' ideas and thoughts which refer to nothing 'external' " (Jung, 1933, par. 747). Perversion, whether sexual or non-sexual, brings the distorted framework of past traumatic relationship to the fore, creating different registers for experiencing the world.

The ectype as an internal (com)poser creates an unconscious conviction that templates all relationships, distorting the whole psychic network. With associated fantasy material, it dominates the form of future relationships, both directly by replicating affective states, and also in a compensatory manner through self-deceptive reversals. Chasseguet-Smirgel (1989, pp. 95–101) describes affective reversal in cases of the projected relationship (ectype) reflecting a perverse mother–child relationship where there may even be dissociation in the form of a fantasised geographical location, a Utopia representing the mother's womb, that offers a compensatory maternal relationship denying both the father and psychic growth. Utopias usually have an island and an enclosed garden within which a child finds an immediate satisfaction of his needs, "establishing a symbiosis with Mother Nature, who offers her children her overflowing breast to the exclusion of the father" (1989, pp. 95–96). The shadow side of this idealistic, compensatory relationship is isolation and stagnation on the desert island of perversion, devoid of the resources to promote a developing or rewarding relationship. This illustrates both the strength of projection and dissociation, through geographical contextualisation, and the compensatory idealisation of the perfectly rewarding, but one-sided relationship.

I suggest that in perversion the projected relationship goes even further, that it enfolds, and is enfolded by, a whole world view that becomes a "position", or underlying constellation (Parsons, 2000, p. 41; see also Chapter Five: The concept of position), from which all relationships are experienced. This whole world view could be described as the opposite, or shadow, of Jung's (1955, par. 704) description of the projection of the image of God to create a psychic world order: it is a malevolent kleptocracy, a world governed, or parented, by thieves. The unconsciously perceived psychic theft is of the child's individuation and possibility of growth towards whole-ness. The revenge is predatory attack and counter-victimisation, steal-ing the right to individuation from others. This model extends the scope of the psycho-analytic theory of vengefulness in sexual perver-sion exemplified in Chapter Four (Aggression and sadism), where Stoller (1977, pp. 96–110) describes sexual perversion as hatred expressed through sexual action in a fantasised revenge for trauma or humiliation in childhood, converting these experiences into triumph. There appears to be no adequate explanation for ring-fencing *sexual* fantasies and acts for this revenge. I am proposing a more insidious and all-consuming unconscious template, dominating both sexual and non-sexual ideation and expression.

Case One—Fred West—sexual perversion

Fred West was a voyeur. Voyeurism was his "type" of perversion. He especially liked watching other men having sex with his wife (Burn, 1998, p. 128). ". . . Watching sex was good. Watching the others get off on the sex without them realizing he was watching was better" (p. 145–146). He also liked watching animals mating (p. 166). He pimped his wife, preferring to procure black men who knew they were doing him a favour and were never asked to pay. He became obsessed with scouting for other men he wanted to have sex with her (p. 107). The compliance of his wife, Rosemary, illus-trates her complementary exhibitionism. West described them as "locked into each other's thoughts" from the first time they kissed (p. 105). West's world had always been a kleptocracy. Those in power took from the vul-nerable. Parents owned their children and took what they wanted from them. In this social system, having sex with one's children was a parental right. West adopted the world view espoused by his parents. Showing a daughter what sex is became "a father's job". Her virginity was his to take (p. 126). He extended this to ownership of their bodies with the right to take their lives as well. This stealing was all-pervasive—he was a kleptomaniac.

He also stole tools and equipment (pp. 125 & 147), tax discs, car parts (p. 197), and bikes (p. 377). He became "... a compulsive pilferer and handler of stolen goods ..." (p. 332). The only reason he ever took his son to the park was to steal other children's bikes (p. 377). His son described him as "the incredible thieving machine" (p. 220).

Case Two—Harold Shipman—bodily perversion

From the seventeen-year-old who was powerless to help his mother or prevent her death, left passively watching the doctor with his ability to alleviate pain, he became compulsively attentive to the sick, wanting to involve himself in all aspects of their lives. As one patient said, "It didn't matter what time you rang up. I had his home phone number and didn't have to wait for the surgery" (Peters, 2005, p. 23). Shipman disavowed his mother's death, becoming more powerful than her doctor in giving himself the power to steal life, and the power over death in becoming Britain's most prolific serial killer.

He appeared omnipotent by getting away with it for so long for, despite suspicions (p. 28), no one else had an overview of the kleptocracy he created—his kleptomania expressed in the stealing of lives and of futures. Although not mentioned by the author, the life / death reversal may not be about killing as such but about the unconscious fantasy of creating life from death. A useful theoretical concept here is one of Matte Blanco's principles of unconscious logic, the principle of symmetry, whereby the system unconscious treats the converse of any relation as identical with the relation. In other words, it treats asymmetrical relations as if they were symmetrical (Matte Blanco, 1975, p. 38). Applying this principle, "mother is dead" is unconsciously equivalent to "dead is mother", and the imposition of death is also the creation of life, in Shipman's case, the life of his mother. Significant factors at the typal level of perverse relationship present as the control over the other in death, the infliction of death through morphine injections (Peters, 2005, p. 120), the psychic equivalence of death and peace, (all Shipman's victims appeared in death as if they had fallen peacefully asleep) (p. 34), the watching of death; the positioning of the body at the time of death (as his mother is thought to have been), and the time of day (nearly always the afternoon, near the time his mother died) (p. 122).

Case Three—Robert Maxwell—emotional and cognitive perversion

Maxwell presented himself to the world as "the super tycoon, a one-man conglomerate who owned newspapers, publishing, television, printing and electronic databases from one end of the earth to another. They knew his name and power in a hundred countries where his assets, on paper, were a staggering £4.2 billion—a figure he never tired of quoting" (Thomas & Dillon, 2002, p. 7). His instructions for his sixty-fifth birthday party were that it "should outshine any other party . . . The great and the good of the world were to be invited . . . Its theme would be his part in world publishing, the emphasis to be on the word 'world' . . . a testament to his 'pre-eminent role' in the fields of technology, science and educa-tion" (p. 171). He made a great deal of his money directly or indirectly through the marketing of a software surveillance product known as *Promis*. Maxwell had the *Promis* disc invisibly microchipped, providing a "trapdoor" that allowed intercepts of all information being tracked by the purchaser of the system (p. 61). When he became a spy for the Israeli secret service agency Mossad (p. 71), he sold *Promis* to the secret services of many countries. He also sold it to Credit Suisse which was unwittingly being used by both the CIA and Mafia in their financial transactions. Within days the adulterated *Promis* software had stolen the numbers of every CIA and Mafia account (p. 78). Maxwell was "wiring up the world for Mossad" (p. 108).

H. Regression moves psychic functioning back, not only through personal emotional development, but to an earlier evolutionary stage of cognitive development in which technical intelligence predominates. This mode of functioning acts subversively through the ectype to transform whole-person relationships into technical relationships

From a Jungian perspective, defences, if regulated, can facilitate psychic development. Frieda Fordham (1959, p. 19) views the defence of regression in this way. If conscious adjustment fails and progression becomes impossible, the libido may flow back into the unconscious which can become overburdened and need to find an outlet. Regres-sion then serves the needs of the unconscious as progression meets the needs of consciousness. Mogenson describes this process archetypally as, "Overwhelming events, which cannot be incorporated into the life we have imagined for ourselves" causing "the soul to bend back on itself, to commit 'incest' with itself, and to revert to the heretical modes of the primary process" (Mogenson, 2005, p. 141). He describes portions of the libido that cannot move forward towards realistic object-cathexis, re-ordering themselves and curing themselves by regressing back into the maternal embrace of the collective unconscious. This is more than regression back to childhood states, or the idealisation of pregenitality (Chasseguet-Smirgel, 1985, p. 141), it is a movement back to areas "anterior to sexuality" (Mogenson, 2005, p. 143), conceptualised as archetypal incest with the Great Mother. In perversion, impairment of the transcendent function means lack of connectivity, preventing the psyche from accessing the healing and curative benefits of the archetypal maternal embrace. Regression to the collective unconscious does operate, but in a destructive and dehumanising way.

As the ectype is infused with perverse ideation, relating to how early trauma was experienced, it becomes associated in each particular individual with a consistent type of sexual or non-sexual perverse behaviour. Greenfield quotes the psychologist William Calvin, who suggests that humans are distinct from all other animals in that they are always, inevitably, "stringing things together in structured ways, ones that go far beyond the sequences produced by other animals" (Greenfield, 2008, p. 163). One such combining into strings is of ". . . elaborate narratives into games with procedural rules" (2008, p. 163). At this stage of perversion such internal strings with procedural rules serve to structure what will now be referred to as a "technical" relationship, the term introduced by Bach (1991, p. 76; see also Chapter Five: Emphasis on object relations).

I have also drawn the term "technical" from the work of the archaeologist Mithen because, while overlapping with the idea of part object relationship, there are different qualities which I wish to convey as essential to the theoretical formulation I am propounding. A relationship based on technique rather than full human quality, is described by Mithen, who draws parallels between the evolutionary development of the mind and child development. He proposes three broad architectural phases for the evolution of the human mind. In phase one the mind is dominated by a domain of general intelligence, which he describes as a suite of general-purpose learning and decision-making rules. This is followed evolutionarily by phase two, in which general intelligence is supplemented by multiple specialised intelligences working in isolation from each other. Finally in phase three, about 100,000–30,000 years ago, these specialised intelligences begin to work together and indicate a flow of knowledge and ideas between behavioural domains (Mithen, 2005, p. 69). When the mind reaches its last phase, equivalent to Piaget's formal operational intelligence, and achieved by children at about twelve years (Flavell, 1963, pp. 204–211), it can think about hypothetical objects and events (Flavell, 1963, p. 35). Mental imagery is important in the designing of tools during this final stage. Mithen (2005, p. 224) conceives of the primitive mind as consisting of three entities: a technical intelligence (producing stone tools), a natural intelligence (understanding of landscape and wildlife), and a social intelligence (skills needed to live in groups), and he points to the seriousness of adequate integration of technical and social intelligence.

Technical intelligence is devoted to thought about physical objects that can be manipulated for any desired purpose: they have no emotions or rights because they have no minds. As the use of metaphor and analogy works mainly across domain boundaries (Mithen, 2005, p. 243), this cognitive fluidity creates the possibility that people can be thought of in the same manner as physical objects and tools. Thus, Mithen's theory could offer an explanatory framework for the ability of the psyche, through evolutionary regression, to depersonalise the other, as happens in perverse relationships. Added to this archaic dimension, there is an unconscious reversal (Matte Blanco, 1975, p. 38) in perversion, so that early traumatic experiences, such as being treated as a less-than-human object, can be reversed and imposed upon another. Matte Blanco (1999, p. 59–61) regards the distinction between symmetrical and asymmetrical logic to be as meaningful a division of the mind as that between conscious and unconscious processes.

This movement away from genuine relationship to technical relationship is an expanding feature in our technological society. Entertaining games can be played in social isolation through interaction with computer characters that represent real people or real creatures. In fact criticism of computer games often centres on the dangers of not having to take the feelings of the other into account, a mode of interacting which can then transfer to human relationships in which people can be treated as objects with impunity. Taken the other way round, when playing a computer game in which *no* images of living creatures appear, the player can still easily project negative feelings onto (non-existent) competitors, such as anger, disappointment, and revenge if the player is winning, or if losing, gloats of satisfaction at the player's humiliation. Putting together these two distorted perceptions, that people and creatures featured in competitive computer games *do not have* real feelings and that computer images *have* real feelings, there emerges an unconscious equivalence of sentient and non-sentient opponents.

Frequent misperceptions of this sort, particularly if reinforced during childhood, could well be associated with a lack of empathy, understanding, and consideration for the other in relationships more generally. Palmer (2007, pp. 7–8) goes so far as to describe modern childhood, dominated by technology, particularly external screen imagery, as "toxic". As could be said of perversion, she considers that it subverts the growth of rewarding relationships because it prevents:

- focusing on other people's choices rather than what grabs your attention
- being able to defer gratification
- being able to balance your own needs against those of others.

Case One—Fred West—sexual perversion

West had a particular modus operandi that subverted whole person relationships, replacing them with a technique. He was able to engage others through his charm. He "had a way with the chat" (Burn, 1998, p. 53); he was "... the sort of man who could talk the birds out of the trees. He had the gift of the gab" (p. 102). However, this is only the icing on his technique. "All through his life he would invest his deepest and most complicated emotions—all his most difficult and disturbing thoughts, not in people, but in things. Places and things. People as things." "He always preferred inanimate objects to breathing, responding—and therefore threateningly dangerous and unpredictable—people. The deadened and dehumanized over the alive and responding". "It was always objects over people. Activity over closeness" (p. 105–106). Women were often objects to be investigated and he liked investigating them internally with a camera (p. 411). His stolen tools were fetishistic objects. "Sex and work. Work and sex. The two mutually contaminating; continually cross-feeding" (p. 127). "He was always waiting for work. He would put his boilersuit on even on a Sunday and if there was no job lined up for him to go to he would start pacing. . . . Backwards and forwards. Up and down" (p. 417). West did not understand the world of people relationships, ". . . he wasn't interested in making any kind of social life" (p. 419). He did understand thing relationships. His murders usually involved a perverse ritual of dismembering the legs, removing the kneecaps and some fingers and toes (p. 173). "In his many weeks of police interviews after his arrest in 1994, he would repeatedly refer to the body of a murdered person as 'it' and to inanimate objects and material and pieces of equipment . . . as him" (p. 175). Buildings also become equivalent to bodies. "When he wasn't at work he was working on the house. Rewiring, replumbing, roofing, digging up floors, pouring new footings" (p. 219). In other words the house was constantly being interfered with. He had a need to explore orifices and holes. Holes in his house were packed with the headless and legless torsos of girls and young women (p. 251). His longest job was as a "driller". He drilled holes using a machine called a Power Thrust. This is a job he took to (pp. 269 & 272). When finally interviewed by the police, "What was striking about Fred West's account of how he murdered and mutilated his daughter was the way in which the close details of exactly how he had murdered and mutilated Heather and disposed of her remains frequently slipped into animated soliloquies of ordinary household things. With a sort of compulsion, a description of cutting and carrying would turn, in one or two sentences, into a hymning or inventorying of the objects he had done the cutting or carrying—or tying or washing or concealing—with" (p. 403).

Case Two—Harold Shipman—bodily perversion

Shipman's patients experienced him as charming. "Even those who are relatives of his victims have stories to tell about what a good doctor he was" (Peters, 2005, p. 22). But this is one side of a "Jekyll and Hyde personality" (p. 33). Shipman conducted his killing like a technical operation using medical equipment and terminology. The victim became an object and, as Paul Britton states, "the killing in itself was not valuable", it was conducted as quickly and efficiently as possible with a syringe as the "tool" (p. 51). Shipman might be compared with Eichmann, a Nazi expert on the "Jewish problem" (Arendt, 2005, p. 5), "a man who lived for his idea . . . and who was prepared to sacrifice for his idea everything and, especially, everybody" (Arendt, 2005, p. 9). By 1995 Shipman's modus operandi changed. He had been killing for over twenty years and he now seemed content to leave the patient he had just murdered before they actually died, and to imagine the moment of death. Paul Britton believes that "Shipman could picture the tableau, the room, and the person he had left. He would be able to visualise how they actually made the transition from being alive to being dead, and how they looked in death" (Peters, 2005, p. 209). In court, he saw himself as a star in his technical medical world, and untouchable by the law. "Shipman clearly could not understand why the witnesses were being called" (p. 103). He showed little interest in the people he had killed but only in the technicalities of the trial (pp. 109–110).

Case Three—Robert Maxwell—emotional and cognitive perversion

Maxwell used people rather than relating to them. Fixated on his own ambitions he would "ignore the view of others if these [were] not compatible" (Thomas & Dillon, 2002, p. 217). He easily lost his temper if people did not do things his way. Once, in a London restaurant, he swept china, glasses, and cutlery to the floor because he did not like the way the table was laid (p. 257). He could also regress in his speech "like an angry infant" (p. 262). "Russia would become 'Wussia' ", and the chef on his boat "needed wessons in how to cook the way I like things" (p. 262). He hired and fired at a whim ignoring the feelings of members of his staff. "A secretary had been fired for overlooking to make sufficient copies of a memo, another sacked for forgetting he took only one spoonful of sugar in his coffee" (p. 44). Throughout much of his marriage he exercised fierce control over his family, "his wife had no direct access to him" (p. 104), none of his children could marry unless he approved their partners (p. 81), and he boasted that he had left them no inheritance (p. 166). He wanted admiration for his power and influence, not for his integrity or honesty in either personal relationships or business dealings. His nickname was the "bouncing Czech" (p. 6).

I. Repetition compulsion, combined with an unconscious reversal in the direction of negative affect, leads to predatory sexual, bodily, emotional, or cognitive enactments whose nature reveals unconscious archetypal domination

Repetition has already been alluded to as having a positive, strengthening role in what is described as psychic homework, meaning the private processing of initially unintegratable, and so untransformable, relational input (Theoretical formulation—C). Repetitive exposure with consideration is a way of addressing a reality that cannot be understood or dealt with when first experienced and, like a repetitive dream, is an inner way of re-experiencing something that needs to be re-experienced in order for it to be better understood.

The movement from healthy repetition to repetition compulsion is a movement from inner to outer, from ideation to behaviour, that could be associated with the inner "compulsion to idealise", regarded by Chasseguet-Smirgel (1974, p. 352) as no less powerful than sexual compulsion. This occurs when inner and outer worlds, or magical and mental levels of consciousness (Ujhely, 2003, pp. 51–52) are not sufficiently differentiated. Whereas on the mental level there is separation and two-ness, on the magical level there is oneness, with the other denied independent existence. On the magical level closeness is sought, on the mental level the only concern is personal affect. Primary process (fantasy) thinking operates and thought processes are acausal, concrete, rigid, and labile.

This path to symptom formation involves what Hillman (1991b, p. 146) describes as reversion into a mythical style of consciousness to escape reality. A concretistic fallacy is adopted, in which there is a lack of distinction between archetypal symbolism and concrete reality, creating a delusional state in which inner symbolic images are experienced as being real, external facts (Edinger, 1973, pp. 110–111). Beebe interprets this as Jung's meaning of the *introverted* use of a psychological function, that is dependent on an "idea". He employs the term idea to express the meaning of a primordial image or archetype (Beebe, 2006, p. 134). An introverted function:

> . . . is one that has turned away from the object and toward the archetypal "idea" that the object might be most closely matched to. This archetypal idea, residing in the inner world, can be understood as a profound thought, a value, a metaphorical image, or a model of reality, depending upon whether the introverted function is thinking, feeling, intuition or sensation. When an introverted function is used to orient to something external, it is in the end the comparison to the archetype not the stimulating object or situation itself, that finally commands the attention of the function. This can seem like a withdrawal from the object itself. (Beebe, 2006, p. 134)

The ectype, together with the type that it parents, becomes the internal form that templates relationships. This form represents the psyche in relationship, encompassing bodily, emotional, and cognitive aspects, with tactically codified, multi-layered encrypted meanings, from consciousness, from the personal unconscious, and from the collective unconscious. The process of symbolisation is now stunted by lack of imagination, and is replaced by a credenda, that is, an inventory of imagery and ideation (Money, 1988, p. 128; see also Chapter Five: Further expansion of the traditional model). This is perversion compliant and combines with harboured negative conjunctive (relational), and often body, memories, to impel expression through somatisation, with action rather than thought (Chapter Six: Psyche/soma). Such perverse bodily expression is a somatic metaphor expressing distressing relational experiences. It becomes a cycle of compulsive action that creates a mimicry of truth, a false truth that looks only for self-referential validation.

Whether consciously or unconsciously elicited, like an IRM, over-prescribed perverse iconography is the trigger stimulating a specific type of action in relation to another person. It represents the extra-verted, behavioural end of the archetype (Chapter Six: Image). This is particularly well known in sexual perversion when orgasmic excite-ment is often dependent upon narrowly prescriptive visual stimuli, prototypically exemplified in the case of fetishistic objects. Whereas the unconscious was traumatically imposed upon, in reversal it now imposes on consciousness, causing a blinkered and compulsive drive from image to action.

The repetition compulsion is also combined with an unconscious directional reversal. Putting together Mogenson's two observations that we repeat what traumatises us and that we repeat it with a parent (Mogenson, 2005, p. 124), the repetition compulsion can be seen as operating through an ectype defining parent–child or domi-nator–dominated relationships. Matte Blanco's (1975, p. 38) principle of symmetry in unconscious logic explains the reversibility of affec-tive direction, so "she harms me" is unconsciously equivalent to "I harm her" although consciously it would be understood as the opposite.

Repetition compulsion with its addictive attachment to behavioural rituals, which in perversion are often aggressive or sadistic (Glasser, 1979, p. 281), serves as a defence of the self (Kalsched, 1998, p. 85). Decontextualisation acts as a protection against learning and change, and is instituted through fear of integrating traumatic or potentially destructive material. The autistic withdrawal and intoxication with compulsive and repetitive behaviour in which the wish represents reality, is motivated by an unconsciously perceived need to protect the psyche; a protection achieved by retaining unintegrated ectypes in one or more dissociated subcentres that structure repetitive behavioural rituals and oppose the establishment of progressive intrapsychic or interpsychic relationships or movement towards wholeness. There is no reference to a moral compass in this extreme development. Desire becomes a mindless appetite. As Spinoza's states, "we neither strive for, wish, seek, nor desire anything because we think it to be good, but, on the contrary, we adjudge a thing to be good because we strive for, wish, seek or desire it" (Spinoza, 2001, p. 107).

This doom-laden defence with repetitious mimicry acts as an algorithm, propelling dissociated psychic content infinitely and soullessly in a circular movement around its own axis. Hillman notes that in archaic western symbolism the circle is a place of death and, "Defensiveness is in the very nature of the circle itself" (Hillman, 1979, p. 160) (The circle as a motif offering this protective power appears as ritual protection marks (RPMs) found in three National Trust properties in Kent: Ightham Mote, The Priest's House at Sissinghurst Castle, and at Smallhythe Place. The marks are usually small circles on fireplaces, bessumers, doors, and windows and are believed to offer protection through the quality of having no beginning and no end, thus denying evil an entry point.)

Case One—Fred West—sexual perversion

West led a compulsive life, driven by an entwined combination of work and sex, with sex often tackled as if it were a work project. This behaviour, including his crimes, testifies to a drivenness. When not working on sexual projects he was working on the "body" of his house (p. 219). His activities were violently attacking and destructive, a reversal of the violence, including sexual violence, of which he was a victim when a child (pp. 141–147). He was the victim turned victimiser who preyed upon the young and vulnerable. The strength and narrowness of his compulsions, his lack of personal relationships or of interest in other aspects of life suggest a domination by archetypal forces beyond his control.

Case Two—Harold Shipman—bodily perversion

Repetition compulsion is evident in the serially applied killing formula of lethal injection employed by Shipman. The inquiry following his conviction for fifteen murders found him responsible for the deaths of more than two hundred and sixty patients (Peters, 2005, p. 75). His technique was sufficiently accomplished for him to kill several patients every month towards the end of his life. The unconscious reversal is demonstrated in the misuse of his powerful position of trust as a GP and the negative affect in his desire to bodily attack those he was appointed to heal.

Case Three—Robert Maxwell—emotional and cognitive perversion

Maxwell's perverse enactments centred round his compulsive ambition for wealth, power, and social position. His serial acquisition of newspapers, in which he regularly featured, promoted this cause while the selling of adulterated *Promis* software (Thomas & Dillon, 2002, pp. 70, 78, 83, 106, 115, & 120) enabled surveillance of competitors on the world stage. His non-stop ruthless acquisitiveness established his status within a "coalition of global criminals" (p. 163). The "Maxwell factor" has been cited as "a significant turning point in the way East European criminals operated" (p. 368), with suspected links to terrorism. Eventually his continuous need for self-aggrandisement, his inability to stop accumulating and consolidate, meant that he overreached himself financially. Although resorting to a raid on the pension funds of his own employees (p. 163), he could not avert the largest bankruptcy in British history (p. 357).

Complete theoretical formulation

The predisposition to perversion presumes a conjunctive affective memory of unbearable relational experience. Initially, the same defensive mechanisms of splitting and projection are used as in non-perverse development, with temporary removal of unintegrated relational material in the form of a psychic sticker, associated with one or more complexes, so that it may be deconstructed and imbued with new meaning.

The work required is that the psyche address the projected imagery and affect on all levels of consciousness, and also as its own experience of the external world. If this process is successful and the material represented by the sticker is sufficiently reintegrated, use of the sticker can be relinquished and further defensive manoeuvres abandoned.

Perversion presumes a failure of this reintegrative process due to either inadequate processing of the projected contents or failure of the ejecting psychic system to develop schemata that can accommodate the projection. If the sticker remains unintegrated, the projected contents can dissociate further and develop as a semi-independent ectype, a subcentre representing the form or idea of perverse relationship.

The perverse dynamics of the dissociated ectype threaten the integrity of the psychic system and command the employment of further defences. Projective defences are strengthened so that the relational content of the ectype is contextualised and becomes typal, producing an unconscious conviction which templates all relationships and is underpinned by the vengeful projection of a kleptocracy as a whole world view of relationships.

Regression moves psychic functioning back, not only in terms of personal emotional development, but to an earlier evolutionary stage of cognitive development in which technical intelligence predominates. This mode of functioning acts subversively through the ectype to transform whole-person relationships into technical relationships. Repetition compulsion, combined with an unconscious reversal in the direction of negative affect, leads to predatory sexual, bodily, emotional, or cognitive enactments whose nature reveals unconscious archetypal domination.

CHAPTER EIGHT

Perversion: present and future

If it be not now yet it will come

Shakespeare, *Hamlet*, Act 5: Scene 2

Freud uses perversion to emphasise the importance of infantile sexuality. His two paradigms of polymorphous perversity and the Oedipus complex bind perversion to sexuality and limit perverse enactments to sexual perversions. From this perspective, perversion is either a developmental failure in sexual development beyond the stage of polymorphous perversity, or a failure to resolve Oedipal conflicts. The psycho-analytic interpretive tradition thereafter establishes a synonymity between the terms "perversion" and "sexual perversion".

Despite some expansion of this interpretation, there is still a tendency for theorising about perversion to become locked in a self-referential, rather than a deconstructive, process. This theoretical encapsulation of the concept, with source, aim, and object entwined with sexuality, discourages attempts to incorporate broader understandings of perversion that might threaten the integrity of the traditional Freudian model. Chapter Four, which demonstrates the clarity and explicitness of the theory of perversion within psycho-analysis, is intended as a springboard for thinking beyond the self-enclosure of a limited sexual theory. Although I describe how moves towards expansion have already begun in psycho-analysis, these appear to build on the implicit assumption that non-sexual perversion results from psychopathology in *sexual* development. My broader theoretical model partially de-eroticises perversion by placing its root structure in more general infantile relational experience, rather than in the area of sexuality alone. This postulation exposes an increased area of infantile vulnerability to perverse development, making perversion a more general developmental disorder.

The value of introducing a Jungian perspective to traditional theory is that it offers the possibility of a broader conceptual framework for perversion than sexuality alone. Such a framework can incorporate a range of etiologies, psychic processes, and behavioural expressions. The four main conceptual differences identified between psycho-analysis and analytical psychology in Chapter Six highlight restrictions in the psycho-analytic model of perversion and provide direction for expansion through reference to the Jungian concepts of psychic energy, the collective unconscious, archetypes, and teleology.

My model presents perversion as deviation from an egalitarian, dialogical, and reciprocal relationship, rather than a deviation from genital sexuality. While retaining its structure, the traditional model can be reinterpreted, with a relational rather than a sexual core. If "relationality" (quality of communication in general) replaces "sexuality", then whole person relationship takes the place of genital sexuality, with sexuality reinterpreted metaphorically to mean intercourse of all kinds, both sexual and non-sexual. Perversion is then disentangled from instinctual sexuality and becomes a persistent deviation in the aim, or from the object, of whole person relating. In other words, the aim of perversion is *not* to encounter the other in a mutually satisfying way, and the object is *not* the other person as a whole but only particulars of the person that excite because they meet specific unconscious requirements which, if met, trigger vengeful and demeaning behaviour.

While accepting and retaining perversion as a defensive psychic structure, in my formulation the defences are functionally different. The splitting and projection of affect and image associated with unbearable relational experience, is described as a diphasic process, moving from healthy development to psychopathology as perversion becomes established. Regression is also differently conceived, activating archetypal processes rather than relating solely to the personal unconscious. Denial, in the form of disavowal, is reinterpreted relationally through two contradictory modes of intercourse, with apparent external conformity to the demands of relationship hiding the emotional investment in relating solely to internal reality.

The qualities of aggression and sadism are prominent in the psycho-analytic model. In the revised model they are somewhat differently conceived as operating to achieve a vengeful unconscious reversal of the relational imbalance in power, to compensate for the humiliation of early trauma. Reaching further than the psycho-analytic model, my formulation presents such early trauma as more generally relational, thereby recognising rather than privileging sexuality. Whereas psycho-analysis focuses on sexual ideation and behaviour, my formulation emphasises images and ideas of relational deception and developmental theft, highlighting Jung's understanding of libido as extending beyond sexuality. It portrays perversion as pervasive, neither inner fantasy nor outer activity, but a theme that affects the whole psyche and permeates all relationships and behaviour. This reinterpretation more adequately addresses the range of psychic functioning and of behaviour that emanates from a perverse psychic structure and allows the terms "non-sexual perversion", "bodily perversion", "emotional perversion", and "cognitive perversion" to be subsumed under the same conceptual umbrella as sexual perversion.

This more comprehensive formulation contributes to the theoretical understanding of perversion within analytical psychology. From a Jungian perspective, perversion is a distortion and disruption of the transcendent function, since it attacks symbolisation and obstructs the process of individuation, including healthy connectedness to the collective unconscious. The formulation also contributes to the theoretical understanding of perversion within psychoanalysis more generally by conceptually allying sexual and non-sexual perversion and implicating early relational trauma in the onset and personal specifications of both. This allows deceptive and destructive non-sexual activities including, for example, crimes of deception, to be considered as sometimes (but not always) emanating from a perverse psychic structure.

If perversion is released from specifically sexual roots, and perverse expression is not considered as exclusively sexual, perversion as a psychopathology is open to reclassification as a subsection of personality disorder in *DSM*. This integration in psychopathology could remove some of stigma associated with the condition and help to open up treatment possibilities. The 2006 British Psychological Society report on *Understanding Personality Disorder* (Alwin, Blackburn, Davidson, Hilton, Logan, & Shine, 2006) gives a general definition of personality disorder as "enduring patterns of cognition, affectivity, interpersonal behaviour and impulse control that are culturally deviant, pervasive and inflexible, and lead to distress or social impairment" (2006, pp. 5–6). The authors conclude that most variation in personality is accounted for by the "Big Five" factors, Openness, Conscientiousness, Extraversion, Agreeableness, and Neuroticism (2006, p. 7). They cite McCrae and Costa (1995) who believe that these dimensions "represent *biologically derived tendencies*, which are instrumental in shaping attitudes, goals, relationships and the self-concept, and influence our interactions with the social and physical environment" (1995, p. 248) (author's italics). The description of the five factors places them invitingly close to archetypal predispositions.

Baron-Cohen has another suggestion for reclassification in *DSM*. He advocates a category of "Empathy Disorders" (Baron-Cohen, 2011, pp. 108–109). He defines empathy as "Our ability to identify what someone else is thinking or feeling, and to respond to their thoughts and feelings with an appropriate emotion" (2011, p. 11). This involves two stages; recognition and response. Although he is not writing about perversion, he divides people lacking in empathy into zero-positive and zero-negative. Whereas autism would be zero-positive, perversion would fall into the zero-negative category (which he associates with borderline personality disorder, psychopathic personality disorder, and narcissism). The value of this approach is its emphasis on relationship rather than symptomatology.

Building on the model

This book is a small beginning. A logical next step would be empirical research offering validation, criticism, and elaboration of the theoretical formulation. Two areas of obvious omission so far are, first, the substantiation of theoretical concepts through first-hand clinical material and, second, the subject of perverse psychopathology in women. Although my conceptual model is applicable to women as well as men, further explanation is required to demonstrate how the perverse psychic structure in women is expressed and how it relates to both the female body and mind (Kaplan, 1991; Welldon, 1988).

Inner and Outer

I have associated perversion with lack of loving care and intimacy in early life. However, it could be dangerous to address this particular pathology through psychotherapeutic means alone. There need to be parallel treatment strategies for perverse *behaviour*, which can be destructive or dangerous and requires control, and perverse *intrapsychic functioning* which can only be modified by understanding and by reparative experiences of closeness, warmth, and empathy. Re-establishment of the power and scope of a disabled transcendent function involves the opening up and facilitating of imaginative capabilities, with recognition of a patient's self-betrayal in sacrificing his individuation to the needs of a perversion. A punitive approach to perversion is likely to be counter-productive since this would reinforce the perpetrator–victim experience. Instead, as Van der Kolk and Fisher (1996, pp. 353–355) describe, successful therapy requires feelings to be aroused and assimilated within a new narrative and different models of relationship.

One area I have learned to be of inestimable value in my own practice, is patients' reconstructions of infantile relational experiences, particularly bodily experiences such as breast feeding and skin-to-skin contact. Other specific areas that might very profitably be addressed are the type of projection and dissociation experienced in the clinical setting, the quality of regression to the level of technical relating, and the relationship between ideation, imagery (including dream imagery), and reported or observed perverse behaviour.

Perversion creates an emotional learning plateau on which psychic processes succumb to addiction and cyclical repetition that obstructs development. Understanding of how this cycle operates in a particular individual would help to direct psychotherapeutic intervention towards appropriate psychic exit routes. Considered from a clinical perspective, perversion recruits a range of defence mechanisms that might be experienced transferentially, and could obstruct treatment. These include particular types of projection and dissociation, as well as deep regression to technically based relationships that deny the other as a whole person. At this archetypal level there is also a psychoid mirroring process, in which the collective unconscious deeply reflects the state of the psyche. Such mirroring is beyond the personal; it inspires timeless, spaceless experiences accompanied by archetypal imagery that may present a self-portrait of the psyche's defensive operations (Kalsched, 1996, pp. 2–5).

This book draws illustrations from biographical, rather than clinical material, that is, reported and documented behaviour rather than observation and experience within a clinical setting. As in psychoanalysis, I have used external behavioural patterns, including verbal behaviour, as pointers to internal states of mind and to underlying psychic structures (Grünbaum, 1986, p. 218), although I have not witnessed these behaviours first-hand. It is therefore appropriate to consider the methodology that might be used for direct clinical investigation of some of the connections described. A constructive method of obtaining clinical support for an expanded theory of perversion including sexual and non-sexual manifestations of a perverse psychic structure, would be the use of practitioner-based focus groups in which analysts or psychotherapists could meet to discuss their understanding of particular patients. Patients could be selected either on the basis of their own reported behavioural manifestations of sexual or non-sexual perversion, or through external documentation of perverse behaviour, which might arise through referral from the criminal justice system. Such behaviour could be categorised as (a) sexual, (b) bodily, or (c) emotional or cognitive perversion. Clinical data from patients displaying behaviour identifiable in this way could then be assessed on an ongoing basis for evidence of a perverse psychic structure. The therapist would need to experience, within the psychotherapeutic relationship, a significant cluster of the characteristics associated with a perverse psychic structure. The structure is described in Chapter Four as an organised system of defences involving denial, splitting, idealisation, regression or fixation, aggression and sadism, addiction and compulsion.

Consideration would need to be given as to how the presence of these qualities might be accurately detected. The patient's acceptance of interpretations could not be used as the criterion in the case of perverse patients as perverse psychic functioning might be associated with contra-suggestibility to interpretations (Wisdom, 1967, p. 50). The insight or authority of the therapist might be perversely challenged due to the patient's unconscious need to reject any attempt to engage in cooperative or fruitful interchange. Wisdom suggests that a solution in this type of case might be for an interpretation to consist of "(i) a hypothesis about the motives contained in the patient's associations; and (ii) a hypothesis about the defence he uses to disguise these motives" (Wisdom, 1967, p. 51). With this consideration, each member of the practitioner group might then need to devise their own criteria for understanding that a particular patient, at some level, was acknowledging an interpretation or finding it meaningful.

A reverse approach would be identification by the therapist of perverse psychic structure, followed by recording of observed or reported perverse behaviour, identifying this as sexual, bodily, or emotional or cognitive perversion through ongoing peer group consultation. This type of research through group assessment and discussion could provide valuable comparative data from a shared patient base and encourage the integration of theory and practice, bringing both knowledge and technique to bear on the psychic reality of perversion (Papadopoulos, 2006, pp. 9–10).

Finally, moving from the human clinical to the wider behavioural field, further comparison might be made between ritualistic behaviour in perversion and ethological studies of animal behavioural patterns such as imprinting and other attachment behaviour associated with critical periods in early development (Burkhardt, 2005). A comparison of the critical imagery of innate release mechanisms in animals, and the imagery and ideation triggering action-specific perverse behaviour in humans, might illuminate the role of archetypal, species-specific factors.

REFERENCES

Adair, M. J. (1993). A speculation on perversion and hallucination. *International Journal of Psycho-Analysis, 74*: 81–92.

Adler, N. (1986). Sublimation and addiction: complementarities and antitheses. *Psychoanalytic Psychology, 3*: 187–191.

Affeld-Niemeyer, P. (1995). Trauma and symbol: instinct and reality perception in therapeutic work with victims of incest. *Journal of Analytical Psychology, 40*(1): 23–39.

Alexander, J., & Friedman, J. (1980). The question of the self and self-esteem. *International Review of Psycho-Analysis, 7*: 365–374.

Alwin, N., Blackburn, R., Davidson, K., Hilton, M., Logan, C., & Shine, J. (2006). *Understanding Personality Disorder*. London: British Psychological Society.

American Psychiatric Association (1973). *Diagnostic and Statistical Manual of Mental Disorders* (2nd edn). Washington, DC: American Psychiatric Association.

American Psychiatric Association (1980). *Diagnostic and Statistical Manual of Mental Disorders* (3rd edn). Washington DC: American Psychiatric Association.

American Psychiatric Association (2000). *Diagnostic and Statistical Manual of Mental Disorders* (4th edn). Washington DC: American Psychiatric Association.

Andre, S. (2006). The structure of perversion: a Lacanian perspective. In: D. Nobus, & L. Downing (Eds.), *Perversion: Psychoanalytic Perspectives: Perspectives on Psychoanalysis* (pp. 109–125). London: Karnac.

Andrews, B., & Brewin, C. R. (2000). What did Freud get right? *The Psychologist, 13*(12): 605–607.

Arendt, H. (2005). *Eichmann and the Holocaust.* London: Penguin.

Arlow, J. A. (1991). Derivative manifestations of perversions. In: G. I. Fogel & W. A. Myers (Eds.), *Perversions and Near-perversions in Clinical Practice* (pp. 59–73). New Haven, CT: Yale University Press.

Astor, J. (1995). *Michael Fordham: Innovations in Analytical Psychology.* London: Routledge.

Astor, J. (2002). Analytical psychology and its relation to psychoanalysis. A personal view. *Journal of Analytical Psychology, 47*(4): 599–612.

Ayto, J. (1990). *Bloomsbury Dictionary of Word Origins.* London: Bloomsbury.

Bach, S. (1991). On sadomasochistic object relations. In: G. I. Fogel & W. A. Myers, (Eds.), *Perversions and Near-perversions in Clinical Practice* (pp. 75–91). New Haven, CT: Yale University Press.

Bair, D. (2003). *Jung: A Biography.* Boston: Little, Brown.

Bak, R. C. (1968). The phallic woman: the ubiquitous fantasy in perversions. *Psychoanalytic Study of the Child, 23*: 15–36.

Baron-Cohen, S. (2011). *Zero Degrees of Empathy: A New Theory of Human Cruelty.* London: Allen Lane, Penguin.

Becker, H. S. (1997). *Outsiders: Studies in the Sociology of Deviance.* London: Free Press.

Beebe, J. (2006). Psychological types. In: R. K.Papadopoulos (Ed.), *The Handbook of Jungian Psychology* (pp. 130–152). London: Routledge.

Blake, W. (2000). Auguries of innocence. In: D. Carabine (Ed.), *The Selected Poems of William Blake* (p. 135). Ware, Herts: Wordsworth Editions.

Bloch, I. [1899](1948). *Marquis de Sade: His Life and Works.* New York: Brittany.

Bloch, I. [1904](1934). *Marquis de Sade's 120 Days of Sodom.* New York: Falstaff.

Bohm, D. (1983). *Wholeness and the Implicate Order* (2nd edn). London: Ark.

Bowlby, J. [1969](1999). *Attachment and Loss: Vol. 1. Attachment* (2nd edn). New York: Basic Books.

Branney, P. (2006). Methods and practices: some new dilemmas. *British Psychological Society. Qualitative Methods in Psychology Section Newsletter, 1*: 2–5.

Briggs, J. (1992). *Fractals: The Patterns of Chaos.* London: Thames & Hudson.

Bright, G. (1997). Synchronicity as a basis of analytic attitude. *Journal of Analytical Psychology*, 42(4): 613–635.

Buber, M. (2000). *I and Thou*. New York: Scribner Classics.

Burkhardt, R. W. (2005). *Patterns of Behaviour: Konrad Lorenz, Niko Tinbergen, and The Founding of Ethology*. Chicago: University of Chicago Press.

Burn, G. (1998). *Happy Like Murderers*. London: Faber & Faber.

Camphausen, R. C. (1991). *The Encyclopaedia of Erotic Wisdom*. Rochester, VT: Inner Traditions International.

Caper, R. (1998). Psychopathology and primitive mental states. *International Journal of Psycho-Analysis, 79*: 539–551.

Capra, F. (1982). *The Turning Point*. London: Wildwood House.

Carr, A. P., & Turner, A. J. (Eds.) (2005). *Stone's Justices' Manual Vol. 3*. London: Lewis Nexis, Butterworths.

Casement, A. (2001). *Carl Gustav Jung*. London: Sage.

Chamorro-Premuzic, T., Furnham, A. & Reimers, S. (2007). The artistic personality. *The Psychologist, 20*(2): 84–87.

Charon, R. (1993). The narrative road to empathy. In: H. Spiro (Ed.), *Empathy and the Practice of Medicine: Beyond Pills and the Scalpel* (pp. 147–159). New Haven: Yale University Press.

Chasseguet-Smirgel, J. (1974). Perversion, idealization and sublimation. *International Journal of Psycho-Analysis, 55*: 349–357.

Chasseguet-Smirgel, J. (1978). Reflections on the connections between perversion and sadism. *International Journal of Psycho-Analysis, 59*: 27–35.

Chasseguet-Smirgel, J. (1985). *Creativity and Perversion* (2nd edn). London: Free Association.

Chasseguet-Smirgel, J. (1989). *Sexuality and Mind*. London: Karnac.

Claxton, G. (1998). *Hare Brain and Tortoise Mind*. London: Fourth Estate.

Coen, S. J. (1992). *The Misuse of Persons: Analyzing Pathological Dependency*. Hillside, NJ: Analytic Press.

Cooper, A. M. (1991). The unconscious core of perversion. In: G. I. Fogel, & W. A. Myers (Eds.), *Perversions and Near-perversions in Clinical Practice: New Psychoanalytic Perspectives* (pp. 17–35). New Haven, CT: Yale University Press.

Coverdale, M. (1549). *Oxford English Dictionary, Vol. XI*. Oxford: Clarendon [1989].

Cowan, L. (1982). *Masochism: A Jungian View*. Dallas, TX: Spring.

Dillon-Hooper, P. (2007). Success with sexual offenders. *The Psychologist, 19*(1): 4.

Dollimore, J. (1991). *Sexual Dissidence: Augustine to Wilde, Freud to Foucault.* Oxford: Clarendon.

Dreher, A. U. (2000). *Foundations for Conceptual Research in Psychoanalysis.* London: Karnac.

Edinger, E. F. (1973). *Ego and Archetype* (2nd edn). Baltimore, MD: Penguin.

Edinger, E. F. (1994). *The Mystery of the Coniunctio: Alchemical Image of Individuation.* Toronto: Inner City.

Eiguer, A. (1999). Cynicism: its function in the perversions. *International Journal of Psycho-Analysis, 80*: 671–684.

Eisner, E. W. (2002). *The Arts and the Creation of Mind.* New Haven, CT: Yale University Press.

Ellenberger, H. F. (1970). *The Discovery of the Unconscious.* New York: Basic Books.

Ellis, H. (1906). *Studies in the Psychology of Sex: Sexual Inversion.* Philadelphia, PA: F. A. Davis.

Ellis, H. (1919). The mechanism of sexual deviation. *Psychoanalytic Review, 6*: 391–423.

Ellis, H. (1927). The conception of narcissism. *Psychoanalytic Review, 14*: 129–153.

Ermann, M. (2005). On perverse thinking: a case vignette. *International Forum of Psycho-Analysis, 14*: 188–192.

Escher, M. C. (2010). *M. C. Escher: 29 master prints.* New York: Barnes & Noble.

Fairbairn, W. D. (1944). Endopsychic structure considered in terms of object-relationships. *International Journal of Psycho-Analysis, 25*: 70–92.

Feldman, S. S., Bak, R. C., & Eidelber, L. (1952). Psychodynamics and treatment of perversions. The American Psychoanalytic Association 1952 Annual Meeting. *Bulletin of the American Psychoanalytic Association, 8*: 300–359.

Filippini, S. (2005). Perverse relationships: the perspective of the perpetrator. *International Journal of Psycho-analysis, 86*: 755–773.

Flavell, J. H. (1963). *The Developmental Psychology of Jean Piaget.* Princeton, NJ: D. Van Nostrand.

Fogel, G. I. (1991). Perversity and the perverse: updating a psychoanalytic paradigm. In: G. I. Fogel & W. A. Myers (Eds.), *Perversions and Near-perversions in Clinical Practice* (pp. 1–13). New Haven, CT: Yale University Press.

Fogel, G. I., & Myers, W. A. (1991). *Perversions and Near-perversions in Clinical Practice.* New Haven CT: Yale University Press.

Fordham, F. (1959). *An Introduction to Jung's Psychology* (2nd edn). Harmondsworth: Penguin.

Fordham, M. (1988). The androgyne: some inconclusive reflections on sexual perversions. *Journal of Analytical Psychology*, *33*: 217–228.

Foucault, M. (1979). *The History of Sexuality, Vol. 1.* New York: Pantheon.

Freud, A. (1936). *The Ego and the Mechanisms of Defence.* London: Hogarth.

Freud, S. (1900a). *The Interpretation of Dreams. S.E., 4.* London: Hogarth.

Freud, S. (1905d). *Three Essays on the Theory of Sexuality. S.E., 7.* London: Hogarth.

Freud, S. (1908d). 'Civilized' sexual morality and modern nervous illness. *S.E., 9.* London: Hogarth.

Freud, S. (1909d). *Notes Upon a Case of Obsessional Neurosis* (The 'Rat Man'). *S.E., 10.* London: Hogarth.

Freud, S. (1911a). Psycho-analytic notes on an autobiographical account of a case of paranoia (dementia paranoides) (Schreber). *S.E., 12.* London: Hogarth.

Freud, S. (1911b). Formulations on the two principles of mental functioning. *S.E., 12.* London: Hogarth.

Freud, S. (1914c). On narcissism: an introduction. *S.E., 14.* London: Hogarth.

Freud, S. (1916–1917). *Introductory Lectures on Psycho-analysis. S.E., 15.* London: Hogarth.

Freud, S. (1919e). A child is being beaten. *S.E., 17.* London: Hogarth.

Freud, S. (1924c). The economic problem of masochism. *S.E., 19.* London: Hogarth.

Freud, S. (1927e). Fetishism. *S.E., 21.* London: Hogarth.

Freud, S. (1933a). *New Introductory Lectures on Psycho-analysis. S.E., 22.* London: Hogarth.

Freud, S. (1941f). Findings, ideas, problems. *S.E., 23.* London: Hogarth.

Freud, S. (1943). Untranslated Freud—(9). Some additional notes upon dream-interpretation as a whole (1925), *International Journal of Psycho-Analysis. 24*: 71–75.

Freud, S. (1950a[1896]). Letter 524 from Extracts from the Fliess Papers, *S.E., 1.* London: Hogarth.

Freud, S. (1961). Letter from Sigmund Freud to Romain Ralland, July 20, 1929. In: E. L. Freud (Ed.), *Letters of Sigmund Freud 1873–1939.* London: Hogarth.

Freud, S. (1974a). Letter from Sigmund Freud to C. G. Jung, February 2, 1910. In: W. McGuire (Ed.), *The Freud/Jung Letters: The Correspondence Between Sigmund Freud and C. G. Jung* (pp. 290–293). London: Hogarth.

Freud, S. (1974b). Letter from Sigmund Freud to C.G. Jung, October 13, 1911. In: W. McGuire (Ed.), *The Freud/Jung Letters: The Correspondence Between Sigmund Freud and C. G. Jung* (pp. 448–449). London: Hogarth.

Frey-Rohn, L. (1974). *From Freud to Jung: A Comparative Study of the Psychology of the Unconscious* (2nd edn). New York: Delta.

Giegerich, W. (2004). The end of meaning and the birth of man: an essay about the state reached in the history of consciousness and an analysis of C. G. Jung's psychology project. *Journal of Jungian Theory and Practice, 6*(1): 1–65.

Gillespie, W. H. (1940). A contribution to the study of fetishism. *International Journal of Psycho-Analysis, 21*: 401–415.

Gillespie, W. H. (1956). The general theory of sexual perversion. *International Journal of Psycho-Analysis, 37*: 396–403.

Glasser, M. (1979). Some aspects of the role of aggression in the perversions. In: I Rosen (Ed.), *Sexual Deviation* (2nd edn) (pp. 278–305). Oxford: Oxford University Press.

Glasser, M. (1998). On violence: a preliminary communication. *International Journal of Psycho-Analysis, 78*: 887–902.

Glover, E. (1933). The relation of perversion formation to the development of reality sense. *International Journal of Psycho-Analysis, 14*: 486–504.

Goldberg, A. (2006). An overview of perverse behaviour. In: D. Nobus & L. Downing (Eds.), *Perversion: Psychoanalytic Perspectives: Perspectives on Psychoanalysis* (pp. 39–58). London: Karnac.

Gordon, R. [1983–1984]. *The Location of Archetypal Experience.* The Guild of Pastoral Psychology, Lecture No. 212. London: Colmore, undated.

Gordon, R. (1993). *Bridges: Metaphor for Psychic Processes.* London: Karnac.

Green, A. (2010). Thoughts on the Paris school of psychosomatics. In: M. Aisenstein & E. Rappoport de Aisenberg (Eds.), *Psychosomatics Today. A Psychoanalytic Perspective* (pp. 1–45). London: Karnac.

Greenacre, P. (1996). Fetishism. In: I. Rosen (Ed.), *Sexual Deviation* (2nd edn) (pp. 79–108). Oxford: Oxford University Press.

Greenfield, S. (2008). *i.d. The Quest for Identity in the 21st Century.* London: Sceptre. Hodder & Stoughton.

Grünbaum, A. (1986). Précis of the foundations of psychoanalysis: a philosophical critique. *The Behavioural and Brain Sciences, 9*(2): 217–228.

Grunberger, B. (1966). Some reflections on the Rat Man. *International Journal of Psycho-Analysis, 47*: 160–168.

Haig, B. (2009). Evaluating explanatory theories. *The Psychologist, 22*(11): 948–950.

Haralambos, M., & Holborn, M. (1995). *Sociology — Themes and Perspectives.* London: Collins Educational.

Hauke, C. (2000). *Jung and the Postmodern: The Interpretation of Realities*. London: Routledge.

Hillman, J. (1964). *Suicide and the Soul*. London: Hodder & Stoughton.

Hillman, J. (1979). *The Dream and the Underworld*. New York: Harper Perennial.

Hillman, J. (1991a). The poetic basis of mind. In: T. Moore (Ed.), *A Blue Fire* (pp. 15–35). New York: Harper Perennial.

Hillman, J. (1991b). Pathologizing: the wound and the eye. In: T. Moore (Ed.), *A Blue Fire* (pp. 142–165). New York: Harper Perennial.

Hirschfeld, M. [1910](1991). *The Transvestites: The Erotic Drive to Cross-dress*. New York: Prometheus.

Hirschfeld, M. [1911](1947). *Sexual Pathology: A Study of Derangements of the Sexual Instinct*. New York: Emerson.

Holmes, E. (2010). Spearman Medal 2010. *The Psychologist*, 23(7): 583.

Hogenson, G. B. (1994). *Jung's Struggle with Freud* (2nd edn). Wilmette, IL: Chiron.

Homans, P. (1989). *The Ability to Mourn*. Chicago: University of Chicago Press.

Jacoby, M. (1993). *Anxiety and the Myth of the Dragon Fight*. Guild of Pastoral Psychology Lecture 243. London: Colmore.

Jacoby, M. (1999). *Jungian Psychotherapy and Contemporary Infant Research*. London: Routledge.

Jaffe, A. (1984). *The Myth of Meaning in the Work of C. G. Jung* (2nd edn). Zurich: Daimon.

Johnson, M. (1992). *The Body in the Mind* (2nd edn). London: University of Chicago Press.

Jones, A. M. (2002). Teleology and the hermeneutics of hope: Jungian interpretation in light of the work of Paul Ricoeur. *Journal of Jungian Theory and Practice*, 4(2): 45–55.

Joseph, B. (1975). The patient who is difficult to reach. In: P. Giovacchini (Ed.), *Tactics and Techniques in Psycho-analytic Therapy. Vol. II Counter-Transference* (pp. 205–216). New York: Jason Aronson.

Jung, C. G. (1908). The Freudian theory of hysteria. *C.W.*, 4: 10–24. London: Routledge & Kegan Paul.

Jung, C. G. (1911). The dual mother. *C.W.*, 5: 306–393. London: Routledge & Kegan Paul.

Jung, C. G. (1913). The theory of psychoanalysis. *C.W.*, 4: 83–226. London: Routledge & Kegan Paul.

Jung, C. G. (1914). On the importance of the unconscious in pathology. *C.W.*, 3: 203–210. London: Routledge & Kegan Paul.

Jung, C. G. (1915). *Psychic Conflicts in a Child*. Foreword to second edition. *C.W.*, *17*: 3–5. London: Routledge & Kegan Paul.

Jung, C. G. (1916a). Psychoanalysis and neurosis. *C.W.*, *4*: 243–251. London: Routledge & Kegan Paul.

Jung, C. G. (1916b). The structure of the unconscious. *C.W.*, *7*: 263–292. London: Routledge & Kegan Paul.

Jung, C. G. (1916c). Prefaces to 'collected papers on analytical psychology'. *C.W.*, *4*: 290–297. London: Routledge & Kegan Paul.

Jung, C. G. (1919). Instinct and the unconscious. *C.W.*, *8*: 129–138. London: Routledge & Kegan Paul.

Jung, C. G. (1921). Definitions. *C.W.*, *6*: 408–486. London: Routledge & Kegan Paul.

Jung, C. G. (1926). Spirit and life. *C.W.*, *8*: 319–337. London: Routledge & Kegan Paul.

Jung, C. G. (1927). Mind and earth. *C.W.*, *10*: 29–49. London: Routledge & Kegan Paul.

Jung, C. G. (1928). The relations between the ego and the unconscious. *C.W.*, *7*: 171–239. London: Routledge & Kegan Paul.

Jung, C. G. (1928/1931). Analytical psychology and 'weltanschauung'. *C.W.*, *8*: 358–381 London: Routledge & Kegan Paul.

Jung, C. G. (1929a). Freud and Jung: contrasts. *C.W.*, *4*: 333–340. London: Routledge & Kegan Paul.

Jung, C. G. (1929b). Commentary on 'the secret of the golden flower'. *C.W.*, *13*: 6–55 London: Routledge & Kegan Paul.

Jung, C. G. (1930). Some aspects of modern psychotherapy. *C.W.*, *16*: 29–35. London: Routledge & Kegan Paul.

Jung, C. G. (1933). The real and the surreal. *C.W.*, *8*: 382–384. London: Routledge & Kegan Paul.

Jung, C. G. (1934). The archetypes of the collective unconscious. *C.W.*, *9(i)*: 3–41. London: Routledge & Kegan Paul.

Jung, C. G. (1936a). The concept of the collective unconscious. *C.W.*, *9(i)*: 42–53. London: Routledge & Kegan Paul.

Jung, C. G. (1936b). Individual dream symbolism in relation to alchemy. *C.W.*, *12*: 41–223. London: Routledge & Kegan Paul.

Jung, C. G. (1937). Psychological factors determining human behaviour. *C.W.*, *8*: 114–125. London: Routledge & Kegan Paul.

Jung, C. G. (1938). *Psychic Conflicts in a Child*. Forward to third edition. *C.W.*, *17*: 6–7. London: Routledge & Kegan Paul.

Jung, C. G. (1939). Conscious, unconscious and individuation. *C.W.*, *9(i)*: 275–289. London: Routledge & Kegan Paul.

Jung, C. G. (1946). The psychology of the transference. *C.W., 16*: 167–323. London: Routledge & Kegan Paul.

Jung, C. G. (1947/1954).On the nature of the psyche. *C.W., 8*: 159–234. London: Routledge & Kegan Paul.

Jung, C. G. (1951a). On synchronicity. *C.W., 8*: 520–531. London: Routledge & Kegan Paul.

Jung, C. G. (1951b). The alchemical interpretation of the fish. *C.W., 9*(ii): 154–172. London: Routledge & Kegan Paul.

Jung, C. G. (1954). On the psychology of the trickster figure. *C.W., 9*(i): 255–272. London: Routledge & Kegan Paul.

Jung, C. G. (1955). The conjunction. *C.W., 14*: 457–553. London: Routledge & Kegan Paul.

Jung, C. G. (1958). Schizophrenia. *C.W., 3*: 256–272. London: Routledge & Kegan Paul.

Jung, C. G. (1967). *Memories, Dreams, Reflections*. London: Fontana Library of Theology and Philosophy.

Kalsched, D. (1996). *The Inner World of Trauma: Archetypal Defences of the Personal Spirit*. London: Routledge.

Kalsched, D. (1998). Archetypal affect, anxiety and defence in patients who have suffered early trauma. In: A. Casement (Ed.), *Post-Jungians Today: Key Papers in Contemporary Analytical Psychology* (pp. 83–102). London: Routledge.

Kalsched, D. (1999). Response to 'the multiple self: working with dissociation and trauma'. *Journal of Analytical Psychology, 44*(4): 465–474.

Kaplan, L. J. (1991). *Female Perversions*. London: Pandora.

Kaplan, L. J. (1995). *No Voice Is Ever Wholly Lost*. New York: Simon & Schuster.

Kernberg, O. F. (1984). *Severe Personality Disorders: Psychotherapeutic Strategies*. New Haven: Yale University Press.

Kernberg, O. F. (1988). Clinical dimensions of masochism. *Journal of the American Psychoanalytic Association, 36*: 1005–1029.

Kernberg, O. F. (1990). *Borderline Conditions and Pathological Narcissism*. New York: Jason Aronson.

Kernberg, O. F. (2006). Perversion, perversity, and normality: diagnostic and therapeutic considerations. In: D. Nobus & L. Downing (Eds.), *Perversion: Psychoanalytic Perspectives: Perspectives on Psychoanalysis* (pp. 19–38). London: Karnac.

Khan, M. M. R. (1979). *Alienation in Perversions*. New York: International Universities Press.

Klein, M. (1975). Envy and gratitude. In: M. M. R. Khan (Ed.), *Envy and Gratitude and Other Works* (pp. 176–235). London: Hogarth.

Knox, J. (2004). Developmental aspects of analytical psychology: new perspectives from cognitive neuroscience and attachment theory. In: J. Cambray & L. Carter (Eds.), *Analytical Psychology: Contemporary Perspectives in Jungian Analysis* (pp. 56–82) Hove : Brunner-Routledge.

Kövecses, Z. (2000). *Metaphor and Emotion: Language, Culture and Body in Human Feeling*. Cambridge: Cambridge University Press.

Kradin, R. L. (1997). The psychosomatic symptom and the self: a siren's song. *Journal of Analytical Psychology*, 42(3): 405–423.

Krafft-Ebing, R. von. [1879](1904). *Textbook of Insanity*. Philadelphia. PA: F. A. Davis.

Krafft-Ebing, R. von. [1886](1944). *Psychopathia Sexualis* (12th edn). New York: Pioneer.

Kutchins, H., & Kirk, S.A. (1999). *Making Us Crazy—DSM: The Psychiatric Bible and the Creation of Mental Disorders*. London: Constable.

Laplanche, J., & Pontalis, J. B. (1973). *The Language of Psychoanalysis*. New York: Norton.

Lawlor, R. (1982). *Sacred Geometry: Philosophy and Practice*. London: Thames & Hudson.

Lipton, S. D. (1977). The advantages of Freud's technique as shown in his analysis of the Rat Man. *International Journal of Psycho-Analysis, 58*: 255–273.

Livingstone, E. A. (Ed.) (2000). *The Concise Oxford Dictionary of the Christian Church*. Oxford: Oxford University Press.

Magill, F. N. (Ed.) (1995). *The International Encyclopaedia of Sociology (Vol. 1)*. London: Fitzroy Dearborn.

Mahlberg, A. (1987). Evidence of collective memory: a test of Sheldrake's theory. *Journal of Analytical Psychology, 32*: 23–34.

Manninen, V., & Absets, K. (2000). The face of fear: castration and perversion. *Scandinavian Psychoanalytic Review, 23*: 93–215.

Martin, E. A. (Ed.) (2003). *Oxford Dictionary of Law*. Oxford: Oxford University Press.

Martins, M. C., & Ceccarelli, P. R. (2003). The so-called "deviant" sexualities: perversion or right to difference? *Presented in the 16th World Congress 'Sexuality and Human Development: from discourse to action'*. Havana, Cuba.

Matte Blanco, I. (1975). *The Unconscious as Infinite Sets*. London: Duckworth.

Matte Blanco, I. (1999). *Thinking, Feeling and Being*. London: Routledge.

Mawson, C. (1999). An escalating perversion re-enacted in the transference. Paper given at conference on *Narcissism and Perversion: Modern Kleinian Perspectives*, University College London, April 1999.

McDougall, J. (1972). Primal scene and sexual perversion. *International Journal of Psycho-Analysis, 53*: 371–384.

McDougall, J. (1978). *Plea for a Measure of Abnormality.* New York: International Universities Press.

McDougall, J. (1985). *Theatres of the Mind: Illusion and Truth on the Psychoanalytic Stage.* New York: Basic Books.

McDougall, J. (1991). Perversions and deviations in the psychoanalytic attitude: their effect on theory and practice. In: G. I. Fogel & W. A. Myers (Eds.), *Perversions and Near Perversions in Clinical Practice* (pp. 176–203). New Haven, CT: Yale University Press.

McDougall, J. (1995). *The Many Faces of Eros.* London: Free Association.

McLeod, J. (2001). *Qualitative Research in Counselling and Psychotherapy.* London: Sage.

McVeigh, K. (2011). Cyberstalking 'now more common' than face-to-face stalking. London: *Guardian Newspapers,* 9 April.

Meier, C. A. (1986). *Essays on the Theories of C. G. Jung.* San Francisco, CA: Lapis.

Meltzer, D. (1979). *Sexual States of Mind.* Perthshire, UK: Clunie Press.

Midgley, M. (2003). *The Myths We Live By.* London: Routledge.

Mithen, S. (2005). *Prehistory of the Mind* (3rd edn). London: Phoenix.

Mogenson, G. (2005). *The Most Accursed Religion: When Trauma Becomes a God* (2nd edn). Putnam, CT: Spring.

Money, J. (1988). *Gay, Straight, and In-between, The Sexology of Erotic Orientation.* Oxford University Press: Oxford.

Money-Kyrle, R. E. (1968). Cognitive development. *International Journal of Psycho-Analysis, 49*: 691–698.

Money-Kyrle, R. E. (1971). The aim of psychoanalysis. *International Journal of Psycho-Analysis, 52*: 103–106.

Moore, N. (1983). The archetype of the way (Part 1). *Journal of Analytical Psychology, 28*(2): 119–140.

Moore, T. (1991). The poetic basis of mind. In: T. Moore (Ed.), *A Blue Fire: Selected Writing by James Hillman* (pp. 15–35). New York: Harper Perennial.

Morgenthaler, F. (1988). *Homosexuality, Heterosexuality, Perversion.* Hillside, NJ: Analytic Press.

Moustakas, C. (1994). *Phenomenological Research Methods.* London: Sage.

Neumann, E. (1954). *The Origins and History of Consciousness.* London: Routledge & Kegan Paul [reprinted London: Karnac, 1989].

Nissan, J. (2007). Getting the gist. *The Psychologist, 20*(7): 418–419.

Ogden, T. H. (1989). *The Primitive Edge of Experience.* London: Karnac.

Olson, I. R, Page, K., Moore, K. S., Chatterjee, A. & Verfaellie, M. (2006). Working memory for conjunctions relies on the medial temporal lobe. *Journal of Neuroscience, 26*(17): 4596–4601.

Oxford English Dictionary (1989). *Volume XI.* Oxford: Clarendon.

Palmer, S. (2007). *Toxic Childhood: How the Modern World is Damaging our Children and What We Can Do About It.* London: Orion.

Papadopoulos, R. K. (2006). Jung's epistemology and methodology. In: R. K. Papadopoulos (Ed.), *The Handbook of Jungian Psychology* (pp. 7–53). London: Routledge.

Parsons, M. (2000). Sexuality and perversion a hundred years on: discovering what Freud discovered. *International Journal of Psycho-Analysis, 81:* 37–49.

Partridge, E. (Ed.) (1958). *Origins—A Short Etymological Dictionary of Modern English.* London: Routledge & Kegan Paul.

Paul, K. (2006). *Kandinsky: The Path to Abstraction.* London: Tate Modern.

Peters, C. (2005). *Harold Shipman: Mind Set On Murder.* London: Carlton.

Phillips, A. (1994). *On Kissing, Tickling and Being Bored* (2nd edn). London: Faber & Faber.

Rangell, L. (1991). Castration. *Journal of the American Psychoanalytic Association, 39:* 3–23.

Read, H., Fordham, M., Adler, G., & McGuire, W. (Eds.) (1979). *General Index to the Collected Works of C. G. Jung.* London: Routledge & Kegan Paul.

Redfearn, J. W. T. (1992). *The Exploding Self.* Wilmette, IL: Chiron.

Redfearn, J. W. T. (1994). Introducing subpersonality theory: a clarification of the theory of object relations and of complexes, with special reference to the I/not-I gateway. *Journal of Analytical Psychology, 39*(3): 283–309.

Riesenberg Malcolm, R. (1999). Reflections on perversion and the narcissistic character. Paper given at conference on *Narcissism and Perversion: Modern Kleinian Perspectives,* University College London, April 1999.

Roncaglia, I. (2007). Qualitative approaches: the process of choice. *British Psychological Society. Qualitative Methods in Psychology Section. Newsletter, 3:* 23–25.

Room, A. (Ed.) (1999). *Cassell Dictionary of Word Histories.* London: Cassell.

Rosenfeld, H. (1971). A clinical approach to the psychoanalytic theory of life and death instincts: an investigation into the aggressive aspects of narcissism. *International Journal of Psycho-Analysis, 52:* 169–178.

Samuels, A., Shorter, B., & Plaut, F. (1986). *The Critical Dictionary of Jungian Analysis.* London: Routledge & Kegan Paul.

Sánchez-Medina, A. (2002). Perverse thought. *International Journal of Psycho-Analysis, 83*: 1345–1359.

Saunders, P., & Skar, P. (2001). Archetypes, complexes and self-organization. *Journal of Analytical Psychology, 46*(2): 305–323.

Savitz, C. (1990). The burning cauldron: transference as paradox. *Journal of Analytical Psychology, 35*(1): 41–58.

Schore, A. N. (2003). *Affect Disregulation and Disorders of the Self.* London: Norton.

Schulz, K. (2010). *Being Wrong: Adventures in the Margin of Error.* London: Portobello.

Sedgwick, D. (1993). *Jung and Searles: A Comparative Study.* London: Routledge.

Senge, P., Scharmer, C. O., Jaworski, J., & Flowers, B. S. (2005). *Presence: An Exploration of Profound Change in People, Organizations and Society.* London: Nicholas Brealey.

Shakespeare, W. (1951). *Hamlet, Prince of Denmark.* In: P. Alexander (Ed.), *William Shakespeare The Complete Works* (pp. 1028–1072). Glasgow: Collins.

Shamdasani, S. (2003). *Jung and the Making of Modern Psychology.* Cambridge: Cambridge University Press.

Sheldrake, R. (1987). *A New Science of Life. The Hypothesis of Formative Causation* (2nd edn). London: Paladin.

Sidoli, M. (2000). *When the Body Speaks.* London: Routledge.

Spence, D. P. (1982). Narrative truth and theoretical truth. *Psychoanalytic Quarterly, 51*: 43–69.

Sperling, O. E. (1956). Psychodynamics of group perversions. *Psycho-analytic Quarterly, 25*: 56–65.

Spinoza, B. (2001). *Ethics.* Ware, Herts: Wordsworth Editions.

Steele, R. S. (1982). *Freud and Jung: Conflicts of Interpretation.* London: Routledge & Kegan Paul.

Stein. L. (1966). In pursuit of first principles. *Journal of Analytical Psychology, 11*: 21–35.

Stein, Robert (1973). *Incest and Human Love.* Dallas, TX: Spring.

Stein, Robert (1976). Body and psyche. An archetypal view of psychosomatic phenomena. *Spring*: 66–80.

Stein, Ruth (2005). Why perversion? 'False love' and the perverse pact. *International Journal of Psycho-Analysis, 86*: 775–799.

Steiner, J. (1982). Perverse relationships between parts of the self: a clinical illustration. *International Journal of Psycho-Analysis, 63*: 241–251.

Steiner, J. (1993). *Psychic Retreats.* London: Routledge.

Stevens, A. (1998). *Ariadne's Clue: A Guide to the Symbols of Humankind.* London: Allen Lane, Penguin.

Stevens, A. (2002). *Archetype Revisited. An Updated History of the Self.* London: Brunner-Routledge.

Stevens, A. (2003). Archetypal theory: the evolutionary discussion. In: R. Withers (Ed.), *Controversies in Analytical Psychology* (pp. 252–264). Hove: Brunner-Routledge.

Stevens, A. (2006). The archetypes. In: R. K. Papadopoulos (Ed.), *The Handbook of Jungian Psychology* (pp. 74–93) London: Routledge.

Stevens, A., & Price, J. (1996). *Evolutionary Psychiatry.* London: Routledge.

Stoller, R. J. (1977). *Perversion: The Erotic Form of Hatred* (2nd edn). London: Quartet.

Stoller, R. J. (1991). The term perversion. In: G. I. Fogel & W. A. Myers (Eds.), *Perversions and Near-Perversions in Clinical Practice* (pp. 36–56). New Haven, CT: Yale University Press.

Thomas, G., & Dillon, M. (2002). *Robert Maxwell: Israel's Superspy.* New York: Carroll & Graf.

Ujhely, G. B. (2003). The magical level of consciousness. *Journal of Jungian Theory and Practice, 5*(1): 49–62.

Van der Kolk, B. A., & Fisler, R. (1996). Dissociation and the fragmentary nature of traumatic memories: overview. *British Journal of Psychotherapy, 12*(3): 352–361.

Verhaeghe, P. (2004). *On Being Normal and Other Disorders: A Manual for Clinical Psychodiagnostics.* New York: Other Press.

Von Franz, M-L. (1974). *Number and Time: Studies in Jungian Thought.* Evanston: Northwestern University Press.

Waddell, M., & Williams, G. (1991). Reflections on perverse states of mind. *Free Associations, 2*: 203–213.

Ware, R. C. (1995). Scylla and Charybdis: sexual abuse or 'false memory syndrome'? Therapy-induced 'memories' of sexual abuse. *Journal of Analytical Psychology, 40*(1): 5–22.

Welldon, E. V. (1988). *Mother, Madonna, Whore.* London: Free Association.

West, M. (2007). *Feeling, Being, and the Sense of Self.* London: Karnac.

Wikipedia (2006). Retrieved from en.wikipedia.org/wiki/Perversion 19/05/06.

Wilde, O. (1893)[1996]. *A Woman of No Importance.* Reading: Penguin.

Wilkinson, M. (2005). Undoing dissociation. *Journal of Analytical Psychology, 50*(4): 483–501.

Williams, M. (1973). The indivisibility of the personal and the collective unconscious. In: M. Fordham, R. Gordon, J. Hubback, K. Lambert, &

M. Williams (Eds.), *Analytical Psychology, A Modern Science* (pp. 76–82). London: Karnac.

Williams, M. (1983). Deintegration and the transcendent function. *Journal of Analytical Psychology, 28*(1): 65–66.

Winnicott, D. W. (1945). Primitive emotional development. *International Journal of Psycho-Analysis, 26*: 137–143.

Wisdom, J. O. (1967). Testing an interpretation within a session. *International Journal of Psycho-Analysis, 48*: 44–52.

Zinkin, L. (1987) The hologram as a model for analytical psychology. *Journal of Analytical Psychology, 32*(1): 1–22.

INDEX

Printed in Great Britain
by Amazon

69861883R00099